WHAT IS A NAZARENE?

Understanding
Our Place
in the
Religious
Community

WES TRACY
STAN INGERSOL

Beacon Hill Press of Kansas City
Kansas City, Missouri

CONTENTS

INTRODUCTION

A Spiritual Home

I love the Church of the Nazarene, vulnerabilities and all. Everywhere I go, I find more to love about this wonderful family of faith that puts its arms around the world and creates homelike churches. We are a covenant community of faith.

Nazarenes everywhere seem to sense that our common faith in Christ, our Wesleyan-Holiness heritage, and our family ties are more important than our regional and cultural differences.

I like the way our Nazarene family treasures the past, where memories of shared service and adversity were carved out. Yet we are not enslaved to the words, methods, and peculiarities of a world that we have outgrown. Rooted in what matters most, we lean into the future, knowing that God shares His creativity with us so that we can give a Christlike shape to the years that are about to be.

I like our sense of humor. For the most part, we don't take ourselves too seriously. Few of us fit the irreverent definition of a Puritan—a person with one constant, overwhelming dread: that someone somewhere is having a good time! The ability to laugh at ourselves—the way we tell the zany antics of our family members at a reunion—is a precious gift.

It hasn't always been popular to be a Nazarene. Most of the early Nazarenes came from the ranks of the poor. They knew about praying down rent money, putting cardboard soles in shoes, wearing hand-me-down clothes, and making pledges on faith and not on cash reserves. Further, our doctrines have often been treated with condescending tolerance, even by other Christians. The idea of being pure in heart and life—holy hands and holy hearts—sounds ludicrous to a society fed on neo-Freudian psychology. To the mildly religious and to our Calvinist friends, entire sanctification sounds insufferably arrogant, and sometimes they tell us so.

Nazarene standards of dress and behavior and our resistance to worldly entertainments have drawn caustic comments "knee-deep in snide" from friend and foe alike. Ever been the brunt of "We don't smoke, we don't chew, and we don't go with the girls that do"? True,

4

some of our number have developed the knack of flaunting what we don't do into an art, and all of us get pinched or punched for it. Legalism is one of our predictable vulnerabilities, you know, particularly if our doctrine of sanctification by faith alone gets off-center or misunderstood by the well-meaning.

But through it all, self-surrender in favor of a Christ-centered life has marked the movement. For us, holiness is a vocation, not a vacation. But that doesn't mean we will be popular. Holiness was jeered, not cheered, when John Wesley called England to prayerful searching for sanctifying grace. When he and his Methodist lay preachers proclaimed perfect love, they became at once the scandal and the blessing of the nation.

Service draws the Nazarene family together. Read the Prison Epistles of Paul and see what was on his mind as he faced death and eternity. He did not write about the stock market or the Super Bowl. He wrote to old friends with whom he had shared projects of Christian service. Nazarenes have joined hands to establish gospel beachheads in nearly 120 countries.

We made our mistakes as an adolescent church. We flirted with legalism more than once. Strange, isn't it, how your strengths often create flip-side vulnerabilities? Our standards of dress and conduct also made us vulnerable. Sure enough, some people acted as if keeping rules saves or sanctifies. Only God redeems and purifies. Being Protestant should teach us that.

Others do not always understand our conduct codes. But we came by them honestly. Our blue-collar origins (that's not negative) caused us to express our social conscience in terms of controlling social vices. Our working-class roots meant that we had little social power. We did not know how to change laws and broker political influence. But we could control and improve our personal conduct. We could avoid smoking, drinking, dancing, movies, and the like. The social conscience of Christians in other social rungs took different forms, though. Middle-class Presbyterians tried to make society more Christian by changing unjust laws and policies. They were at home in the halls of power when we were not. They were corporate presidents, bankers, governors, and presidents. Compared to passing a fair labor or race law, avoiding the pool hall was trivial. But we are more mature now; our social concerns go beyond (but do not exclude) personal ethical conduct.

In our adolescence we also flirted coquettishly with Fundamentalism. While we believe in traditional Christianity, we believe there is something better than the extremes of the rigid Fundamentalism of our day. We think there is something better than single-issue politics, see-it-my-way-or-else theology, and lowest-common-denominator church-manship. We prefer the inclusive spirit of our Wesleyan heritage that takes root in the broad Christian tradition, not in sectarian dogmatism. The revival of interest in a full-orbed Wesleyan heritage that marries personal religion and social responsibility has been a defining event in our church.

Another vulnerability arose from one of our strengths. We rightly taught that the Christian is to live above willful sins. But we allowed our challengers to push us so far in the direction of "sinless perfection" that many of our people lost the art of confession. Saved and sanctified people do not have to sin, but sometimes they do. The only thing for Christians to do when they wake up with sin on their hands is to confess it to God. Calling it by another name is no good. But some of our people made mistakes here. Even corporate prayers of confession were deleted from the worship services. It has been a hard lesson to learn. But we have discovered that John Wesley knew what he was doing when he advised even the most holy to properly pray the Lord's Prayer, including "Forgive us our trespasses." That does not mean the believer has committed deliberate sins; but all of us are members of a fallen race, and even our best effort leaves us needing the blood of Christ to atone for unwitting errors and failures of "a thousand infirmities."

We have learned a lot, as any adolescent denomination would. We are now better prepared than ever. Our doctrine of radical optimism, the cleansing from inner sin, is more needed than ever before. Some say that the Church of the Nazarene was raised up not for the 20th century but for the 21st. We have a key contribution to make in the postmodern world.

Not everyone can be won by Nazarenes. Not every Christian would make a good Nazarene. But our Wesleyan-Holiness message of the radical optimism of grace is what our world needs most. Few others believe, as we do, that there is almost no limit to the good things that can happen in and through you because of the atoning grace of Jesus Christ. Social scientists say that personality is formed by age three, or even sooner. They declare that a bad home or neighborhood marks a person forever. We believe in miracles of grace, including the miracle of a pure heart re-created in the image of Christ! Some Protestant friends believe that there is no deliverance from the inner sinfulness of the human heart. Not even the atonement of Jesus, they say, can do that. We must struggle against sin all our lives. But we believe in the miracle of entire sanctification.

Wherever I hear a Nazarene choir sing, hear a Nazarene pastor preach, visit a college chapel service, or enjoy the delights of a potluck dinner, I know I am with people who take to heart our Savior's call to holiness of heart. I look at their faces and know they have met the Lord in a saving encounter. They grieve when they fail and make the pursuit and possession of sanctifying grace life's chief priority. No casual sinning, no cheap grace, no glib discipleship here—these are Nazarenes.

I love the Church of the Nazarene. I think I understand her heart. But I appreciate other Christian traditions as well. Many of them have contributed to our identity. Some do things well at which we are mediocre.

We need to understand that Christian denominations or churches have predictable strengths and vulnerabilities. Christian groups who stress predestination will have problems about the lack of daily holy living among their members. On the other hand, those who stress holy conduct to the point of diminishing grace will predictably be vulnerable to legalism. Denominations for whom ecstatic spiritual experience becomes all in all will produce a shortage of critical thinking among their disciples. Groups who seem to think that ancient ceremonies produce salvation by the church's authority, or that conversion consists of memorizing a catechism, should beware of trivializing a personal relationship with God or an instantaneous conversion experience.

That's why this book was written. In a day and age of consumer Christianity, it's important to understand and preserve an identity.

My coauthor is a third-generation Nazarene on both sides of his family. He joined the church at Ponca City, Oklahoma, at age nine. I've been involved in a Nazarene church somewhere in the world since I was three weeks old. My parents named me after John Wesley and took me as a baby to the Church of the Nazarene in Howard, Kansas. That is where they were saved under the preaching of evangelist A. F. Balsimeier.

I love this Nazarene family that has nourished and nurtured me all my life. I want our church to make the best possible contribution to the times in which we live. Understanding our brothers and sisters in Christ is a start.

—*Wesley D. Tracy*

PART 1

WHO ARE THE NAZARENES?

AT A GLANCE

THEY SHARED A DREAM:
THE LAUNCHING OF THE NAZARENE
MOVEMENT

Historical Background

From roots in the Wesleyan revival in 18th-century England, the Holiness Movement blossomed in America. Wesleyan-Holiness denominations sprang up in every section of the country. Three such denominations joined in 1907 (in Chicago) and 1908 (in Pilot Point, Texas) to form the Church of the Nazarene. Key leaders were Phineas F. Bresee, C. B. Jernigan, H. F. Reynolds, and C. W. Ruth, among others.

Core Beliefs

The dream that drew the founders together was a believers' church in the Wesleyan tradition. This was fleshed out with firm beliefs in orthodox Christianity. Traditional doctrines marked the new Nazarene denomination. These included the inspiration of the Bible, the Holy Trinity, the deity of Christ, and Protestant beliefs in Scripture alone as the Rule of faith and practice, salvation by grace alone through faith alone, and the priesthood of all believers.

The Wesleyan doctrine of salvation, particularly that of entire sanctification, became the foundation for theology, worship, evangelism, nurture, service, and church administration.

The new denomination also stressed education, ordination of women, solidarity with the poor, daily holy living that avoided wicked or worldly practices, and global missionary vision.

The Nazarene founders wanted a believers' church that was rooted firmly in the Wesleyan tradition.

CHAPTER 1

THEY SHARED A DREAM: THE LAUNCHING OF THE NAZARENE MOVEMENT

NINETEENTH-CENTURY AMERICA was a hotbed of religious chaos. False prophets slandered one another and prospered. Zany new religions flourished. Flamboyant spellbinders called themselves evangelists and mesmerized the simple with threats and promises that God, they bellowed, had endorsed. "Farmers became theologians, offbeat village youth became bishops, odd girls became prophets."[1] The times produced eccentricities such as Mormonism, Christian Science, and Jehovah's Witnesses.

The Wesleyan-Holiness Movement was not immune to the stresses. Divided by race and region, it floundered at the edge of a sectarian snake pit by the dawn of the 20th century. Yet from this doubtful setting, the Church of the Nazarene arose, rooted in orthodox Christianity and guided by a vision.

It originated as a *believers' church in the Wesleyan tradition*. "Believers' churches" are distinctive. They are voluntary fellowships of those who experience the regenerating power of divine grace. Their members form a covenant between God and one another and are active in Christian works. They do not allow obvious sin among the clergy and laity to slide; rather, they practice church discipline. They give willingly to the poor and follow a simple pattern of worship. And "they center everything on the Word, prayer, and love."[2]

But for the founders, it was not enough merely to have a believers' church. They wanted a believers' church *rooted firmly in the Wesleyan tradition*, oriented theologically toward landmark doctrines of original sin, jus-

11

tification and sanctification wrought by grace through faith, and the clear witness of the Spirit to the distinct works of divine grace in our lives.

Francis Asbury, founder of American Methodism, had shared the same dream. In 1784 Methodism had an exceedingly small share of the American religious public, but by 1850 it was the largest denomination in America, its growth driven by great engines of revivalism and dedicated circuit riding preachers. It also fell victim to its own success. It excelled at reaching the unconverted but drew them in faster than it could steep them in Wesleyan doctrine, and its identity slowly changed. Eventually the Nazarene founders stepped aside from Methodism.

Unity in Holiness

The vision for bringing the Church of the Nazarene together was centered in a movement with many leaders: Phineas F. Bresee, C. B. Jernigan, H. F. Reynolds, J. B. Chapman, E. E. Angell, and C. W. Ruth, whose revivals for the National Holiness Association took him to every corner of America. Their unflagging efforts united three Holiness denominations and portions of two other groups in a series of steps culminating in the uniting General Assemblies in Chicago (1907) and Pilot Point, Texas (1908).

What distinguished this united church from others?

1. Women joined men in its ministry. Women were eligible for every office in the new church. The ordination of women was a common practice in the three major parent bodies, and women were ordained at both uniting General Assemblies. It was no secondary issue. Bresee insisted that a ministry inclusive of women is *apostolic*, while one that excludes women from ministry is not apostolic.[3] The key scripture was Acts 2:16-17. Men and women share in proclaiming the gospel in the church that moves by the power of the Holy Spirit!

2. The new church stood shoulder to shoulder with the poor and broken. Orphanages in North America and India, homes for unwed mothers, rescue missions for alcoholics—these were visible expressions of inward holiness. "We want places so plain that every board will say welcome to the poorest," Bresee wrote from Los Angeles, while half a continent away Mary Lee Cagle preached to prisoners—Black and White alike—in an Arkansas prison.[4] The early Nazarenes listened with their hearts to "The Spirit of the Lord is upon me, because he hath anointed me to preach the gospel to the poor" (Luke 4:18, KJV). An identification with the Lord's own mission had led Wesley to England's prisons, slums, and mining communities. Now it was the Nazarene founders' concern. Holiness builds a church with a heart for the poor and broken!

3. The early Nazarenes were energized by a vision of worldwide ministry. In 1908 Nazarenes were already ministering in Cape Verde, India, and Japan. They soon did the same in Central and South America, Africa, and China. Evangelism, education, and compassionate ministries were their characteristic methods. Mission stations, preaching points, Bible women, colporteurs, schools, clinics, hospitals, and printing presses were dedicated to the global spread of the Wesleyan-Holiness revival.

4. The Christian college was an essential ingredient of a Wesleyan-Holiness church. The united church began with more colleges than it could support and had to consolidate them. Nazarene communities grew up around these colleges, and some parents moved their families to these communities so that their children could enjoy the benefits of a Nazarene education.

5. Vital piety. The Nazarene prayer meeting, testimony service, and altar service were among the ways that the concern for personal, vital piety would be communicated to a new generation. The experience of God's transforming grace lay at the heart of the Nazarene movement.

6. Entire sanctification was the doctrinal capstone. The uniting core was the idea of a believers' church in which God's grace was real in human lives. Justifying and sanctifying grace were central in the experience and thought of the founders, who knew personally the transforming nature of this grace.

Entire sanctification represented a real cleansing—a true grace in this life—that conquers sin. Every other Christian doctrine was somehow related to this one, and no method could be employed that contradicted it. The deep awareness of sin, repentance, the regenerating power of the new birth, life in the Spirit, true Lord's Supper celebration—all were related to entire sanctification.

The second work of grace was the doorway behind which lay rooms of further experience and life. The founders walked through the door and into the rooms.[5] And if they were still living, they would bid us to follow.

7. Commitment to righteous living. Early Nazarenes agreed that holy living was an important part of Christian stewardship and witness. They committed themselves to daily avoid the wicked and worldly. How could one be a true disciple and have a lavish, worldly lifestyle?

They adopted John Wesley's three rules for the Methodist societies and drew up further rules to guide them. They agreed to avoid entertainments, personal habits, vices, dress, and behavior that would conflict with Christian simplicity.

Keeping rules could not save them. But they knew that ethical conduct is important when it comes to stewardship, discipleship, and witness.

At a Glance

What Nazarenes Believe and Practice

Historical Foundations

The foundation stones on which the Church of the Nazarene is built are five:

Classical Christianity—the religion of the New Testament and the Early Church

Protestantism—the Reformation doctrines, including the priesthood of believers, the Bible as the rule of faith and practice, and salvation by grace alone through faith (not by good works)

Arminian Thought—Jesus made atonement for all. By free grace, each person can choose God and good. Our choice makes a difference; we are not irrevocably predestined either to salvation or damnation.

Wesleyan Practical Theology—adopting and adapting John Wesley's system of doctrine and pastoral theology, Nazarenes continue to emphasize Wesley's distinctive doctrine of entire sanctification.

Holiness—the revival of Wesleyan teachings on sanctification and Christian perfection that swept across 19th- and early 20th-century America was called the American Holiness Movement. The Church of the Nazarene was at the heart of this movement.

Core Beliefs

Nazarene beliefs are founded first of all in the Bible and classic Christian doctrines. Our Articles of Faith descend from the Thirty-nine Articles of Religion of the Church of England as amended and abridged by John Wesley into the Twenty-five Articles of Methodism. From this foundation, the Nazarene Articles of Faith and Agreed Statement of Belief are drawn.

The Nazarene General Rules are taken directly from John Wesley's general rules for the Methodist societies. Our Special Rules attempt to relate Wesleyan-Holiness principles to daily life.

The Church of the Nazarene Today

Today 1.2 million Nazarenes worship in 11,857 congregations in 116 countries and world areas. We have 59 schools of higher education serving 26,000 students. We have 100 compassionate ministry centers and 700 Good Samaritan churches. The Church of the Nazarene believes it has been raised up to carry on in Christ's name worship, evangelism, nurture, and service.

CHAPTER 2

WHAT NAZARENES BELIEVE AND PRACTICE

THE CHURCH OF THE NAZARENE IS A
Christian,
Protestant,
Arminian,
Wesleyan,
Holiness
community of faith. And our creedal statements show it. Our Articles of Faith, Statement on the Church, Agreed Statement of Belief, and General Rules can be found in the appendix of this book and, of course, in fuller form in the *Manual, Church of the Nazarene.*

The Church

The Church of the Nazarene does not fall into the trap of claiming to be the one true Church. Many churches, sects, and cults today make this claim. But Nazarenes nip such extremism in the bud by declaring first of all, "The Church of God is composed of all spiritually regenerate persons" (*Manual, Church of the Nazarene, 1997 — 2001*, par. 23).[1]

This statement marks us as a "believers' church." The Agreed Statement of Belief declares that "the right and privilege of persons to church membership rest upon the fact of their being regenerate" (saved, converted, or born again). The Nazarene *Manual* describes church members as people "who have voluntarily associated themselves together" (par. 25).

Our Articles of Faith accent the Church of the Nazarene as a family of faith. Such phrases as "the community that confesses Jesus Christ as Lord," "the covenant people," "in the unity and fellowship of the Spirit," and "mutual accountability" (par. 15) mark us as a believers' church, a biblical faith community, and also point to the societies, classes, bands, and mentoring pairs in our Wesleyan heritage.

Classical Christians

Several of our Articles of Faith place us squarely in the orthodox, historic, classical Christian tradition. For example, our first three articles about the triune God, Jesus Christ, and the Holy Spirit show that we accept the classic Christian doctrines of the Holy Trinity. "He, as God, is Triune in essential being, revealed as Father, Son, and Holy Spirit" (par. 1). We also affirm our faith in Jesus Christ as "very God and very man, the God-man" who "died for our sins" and "truly arose from the dead" (par. 2). The Holy Spirit is not just the *energy* or *influence* of God, but the blessed "Third Person of the Triune Godhead" who convicts sinners, "regenerating those who repent and believe, [and] sanctifying believers" (par. 3). Thoroughly Trinitarian, we disagree with those who renounce the doctrine of the Holy Trinity, such as Mormons, Jehovah's Witnesses, Muslims, and some Pentecostal groups.

Our articles of faith about the second coming of Christ (XV) and resurrection, judgment, and destiny (XVI) also connect us with classic Christianity. We teach that "the finally impenitent shall suffer eternally in hell." But we also affirm that "glorious and everlasting life is assured to all who savingly believe in, and obediently follow, Jesus Christ our Lord" (par. 22). Our beliefs in the return of Jesus Christ, the resurrection of the dead, a final judgment, and eternal rewards and punishments (pars. 19-22) point not only to harmony with the Scriptures but to the ancient creeds of the Church. Thus, the Apostles' Creed and the Nicene Creed are often used in Nazarene worship.

Protestant Christians

Three of our Articles of Faith identify us with the values defended by the 16th-century Protestant Reformers. Article IV aligns us with the principle of *sola scriptura.* For the first Protestants and for us, *only the Bible* is the divinely inspired Revelation of the "will of God concerning . . . all things necessary to our salvation, so that whatever is not contained therein is not to be enjoined as an article of faith" (par. 4). We believe that neither church leaders nor church tradition speak with as much authority as the Bible.

We celebrate only two sacraments. This number also marks us as Protestants. One is Christian baptism (par. 16). We do not believe that baptism has regenerative powers. Rather, it is "a sacrament signifying acceptance of the benefits of the atonement of Jesus Christ, to be administered to believers. . . . Baptism may be administered [among Nazarenes] by sprinkling, pouring, or immersion" (par. 16). Though Nazarenes usually practice adult "believers'" baptism, the baptism of infants is also provided for in both creed and ceremony (pars. 16, 800.2). "Young children may be baptized, upon request of parents or guardians," says the article of faith. Most Nazarenes today practice infant dedication. But infant baptism was a common practice among early Nazarenes. At the annual district assemblies, the general superintendents often baptized babies. The records show that Phineas F. Bresee, Hiram F. Reynolds, R. T. Williams, J. B. Chapman, and John W. Goodwin often performed these services.[2] We really believe in "liberty of conscience" when it comes to baptism.

Our article of faith on the Lord's Supper has linguistic and theological roots in the Anglican branch of Protestantism. We see Holy Communion as a "memorial" of the sacrificial death of Jesus Christ. Thus, "the bread and wine" are seen as symbols or "emblems of His broken body and shed blood" (par. 802). This places us closer to the Reformed side of Protestantism than to the Lutheran side. Lutherans hold that the literal presence of Christ is in, with, and under the bread and wine.

In the Communion service, Nazarenes examine their hearts before God, meditate on "the death and passion of our Lord," and look forward to the return of Jesus (pars. 17, 802). Some denominations permit only members of the local congregation to partake of the Communion feast, but Nazarene churches invite all believers to share in the Lord's Supper regardless of denominational affiliation. It is, after all, the Lord's table.

Arminian, Wesleyan, Holiness Christians

James Arminius, a Dutch pastor who preached from Romans every Sunday for 13 years, had a profound influence on Protestantism in general and the Wesleyan tradition in particular. Arminius became the spokesperson for those who felt that Protestant leaders like John Calvin and his followers had driven the theological train past the station.

The Protestant Reformers taught that no pope or church could forgive sins or say who is saved—God alone does that. Further, they said—pushing the envelope too far for Arminius—God predestines who is to be saved and who is to be lost. Nothing a person does can change or affect what God decrees. A sovereign God, not the church or its clergy, makes all the decisions.

This became standard Calvinistic doctrine: Jesus died for the elect, those predestined to be saved; all others pay for their own sins in hell. "Limited atonement" is this doctrine's official name. "Irresistible grace" was another cast-in-stone doctrine, which meant that those predestined to be saved cannot change what God has determined to do for them. One fruit of this was the idea of the eternal security of the believer: once God has elected to save you, you cannot fall from His grace. So the Calvinists claimed.

James Arminius, though fiercely opposed for it, preached that Jesus died for all, that all could be saved, and that human beings were given free grace. Further, one had to choose God and good to be saved.

John Wesley (and others) then built a theology that expanded on Arminius. Wesley modified the Thirty-nine Articles of the Church of England, producing Methodism's Twenty-five Articles of Faith. Early Nazarenes, part of the American Holiness Movement, adopted much of Wesley's affirmation of faith.

These are reflected throughout our creedal statements, particularly in Articles V through X. These deal with sin (original and personal), atonement, free moral agency, repentance, justification, regeneration, adoption, and entire sanctification.

We will not unpack these faith affirmations here. You'll see them interpreted throughout this work as Nazarene doctrines are compared and contrasted with other Christian beliefs. You are urged to study these articles in the *Manual* or in this book's appendix. Nevertheless, a few comments will highlight distinctive Wesleyan-Holiness teachings.

If you live in Florida or Louisiana, how many words do you need for snow? Probably only one. Alaskan Inuits, however, have 12 words for it: one for falling snow, another for snow already on the ground, still another for blowing snow—plus 9 more.

How many words does a Christian need for sin? If you're a Calvinist, one may do it—any falling short of God's perfect standard is sin. If you're a Catholic, you need at least two: venial and mortal. If you're a Wesleyan-Holiness Christian, you need a lot of qualifying words for sin, as in inbred sin, sin as act, sin as state, sin of surprise, sin of infirmity, sin of intention, sin of omission, and most of all, sin as a *willful* transgression of a *known* law of God. Probably you could say that Nazarenes are the Eskimos of the doctrine of sin.

Our fifth article of faith carefully spells out the difference we see between original sin and personal acts of sin. We stand clearly in the Augustinian camp, believing that we're born in sin. "We believe that original sin, or depravity, is that corruption of the nature of all the offspring of Adam by reason of which everyone is very far gone from original righteousness" (par. 5.1). Our Arminian roots, however, keep us from proclaiming that total depravity has destroyed everything good in the human heart. Arminianism insists on free grace. Wesleyan dogmatism insists that there are some remains of the image of God in the worst of persons because of prevenient grace. That persuades us to teach that although we are born sinners, we also can find something at the very core of our nature that is positive, godlike, something that can be counted on to seek God and good.

This brings us to Article VII, free agency. When we preach free will, we don't mean the uninhibited freedom that New Age thought or certain psychologies teach. We mean that in the moral realm we have freedom to choose. We have been enabled by prevenient grace (Wesley's term) to choose God and good. Many Christian traditions deny this. But it is part and parcel of the *free grace for all* preached by Arminius, Wesley, and our Nazarene forebears.

Entire sanctification is treated in Article X. This doctrine announces the radical optimism of grace preached by Wesley and his theological offspring. We recognize that people are not impervious to negative environmental forces such as poverty, racism, parental abuse, or deep personal sin. Yet we believe and teach that through the riches of Christ's atonement, there is almost no ceiling on the good things that can happen to anyone. Our gift to this dark age is the good news of entire sanctification.

This article cites a doctrine that distinguishes Wesleyan-Holiness people from others who use the "Holiness" label. Some groups teach holiness as a baptism of the Spirit that empowers the believer for service—but they don't believe that depravity or inbred sin is cleansed. Our article of faith declares that entire sanctification (or the baptism with the Spirit) includes "cleansing of the heart from sin" (par. 13). We take the Bible seriously when it calls believers to be cleansed from "all filthiness of the flesh and spirit" (2 Cor. 7:1, KJV). Nazarenes believe John was serious when he wrote about the blood of Jesus cleansing us "from all sin" (1 John 1:7, KJV). James calls on double-minded believers to "purify your hearts" (4:8).

The article of faith on divine healing (XIV) is our shortest faith affirmation. It represents the reaction of the Holiness Movement to the "healing revival" that broke out early in the 20th century. This article simply states our belief that God does, according to His will, intervene and heal people. But those movements, mostly within Pentecostal and Christian Science circles, carried healing to such an extreme that medical attention was forbidden, causing the Nazarenes to declare pointedly that they believed in both divine healing and medical treatment.

Anointing the sick and calling the elders to pray is an accepted practice among Nazarenes.

The General and Special Rules

Our General Rules (par. 27) are the same three rules that John Wesley created for the early Methodists. Those who wish to join our fellowship "shall show evidence of salvation from their sins by a godly walk and vital piety" and shall "evidence their commitment to God" (27) by the following:

1. "By doing that which is enjoined in the Word of God . . . our rule of both faith and practice" (27:1). This is explained as loving God with all one's heart, soul, mind, and strength and one's neighbor as oneself. Being courteous, helpful, and active in compassionate ministry, supporting the ministry, and faithfully attending church are also cited.

2. "By avoiding evil of every kind" (27.2). Swearing, Sabbath breaking, sexual immorality, quarreling, dishonesty in business or life, pride in dress or behavior, and music, literature, and entertainment that dishonor God are proscribed.

3. "By abiding in hearty fellowship with the church . . . its doctrines . . . and [being] actively involved in its . . . witness and outreach" (27.3).

The Special Rules

The Special Rules (pars. 33-41) represent the church's effort to interpret and apply its Articles of Faith and General Rules to specific needs of a changing culture. Currently, the Special Rules speak against all "entertainments that are subversive of the Christian ethic" (34.1): gambling, membership in oath-bound secret organizations, social dancing, using tobacco or intoxicating drinks, divorce, abortion, and sexual perversions such as homosexual activity or pornographic uses of sex in marriage (34.2-37). The Special Rules speak in favor of Christian marriage, sex as a gift of God, Christian stewardship, storehouse tithing, and support of pastors and other ministers.

What Nazarenes Are Doing in Our World

The Church—and the Church of the Nazarene—has just four things to do: worship, evangelism, nurture, and service. Armed and energized, Nazarenes everywhere busily carry out their fourfold task.

Worship

Nothing more important ever happens on earth than the worship of God. Worship is our first privilege and duty. Whatever else the church is, it is a called-out, worshiping community. Maria Harris wrote, "One Christian is no Christian; we go to God together or we do not go at all."[3] The Christian life is a community affair. Private and public worship are as essential as food and breathing. Today 1.2 million Nazarenes carry out the mission of worship in 11,857 congregations on 340 districts located in 116 countries and world areas.[4]

Those who plan and lead Nazarene worship services have freedom. Unlike such churches as the Greek Orthodox Church that have a precise mandatory liturgy for every Sunday of the year, no prescribed Nazarene liturgy exists. A wide range of worship styles may be found among us from low-church liturgical to very free and spontaneous worship.

The key elements in Nazarene worship include singing, prayer, reading of Scripture, receiving tithes and offerings, and preaching.

Music is a great part of Nazarene worship and will often include piano, organ, or other musical instruments. Sometimes choirs or smaller groups will sing, but always there will be congregational singing. What a privilege to join with fellow pilgrims and, shoulder to shoulder, sing:

> *O Thou in whose presence my soul takes delight,*
> *On whom in affliction I call,*
> *My Comfort by day and my Song in the night,*
> *My Hope, my Salvation, my all!*
> —Joseph Swain

Prayer by clergy and laypersons is part of most Nazarene worship services. Invocations, benedictions, pastoral prayers, laypersons leading in extemporaneous prayer, reciting the Lord's Prayer, open-altar prayer, sentence prayers, directed prayers, and prayer at the altar at the close of an evangelistic service—all of these are integral parts of Nazarene worship.

The public reading of the Bible is included in most Nazarene services. Usually this consists of Scripture reading other than just the reading of it from the preacher's text.

No Nazarene service is complete without the chance to bring our tithes and offerings in support of the church around the world. To us, this is an act of worship.

Preaching is in the anchor position in most Nazarene services— and rightly so. Our churches are pulpits of wood and stone, not shrines or altars of wood and stone. Our pastors are preachers first and priests second. Like the Puritans, we tend to regard the sermon as the "sacrament of the Word."

Preaching has a high place in Christian tradition. Dietrich Bonhoeffer declared, "The proclaimed Word is the Incarnate Christ himself. . . . The preached Christ is the historical Christ and the present Christ . . . walking through his congregation as the Word."[5] "So identified is Jesus the Word with the word of preaching," writes Richard Lischer, "that the one proclaimed once again becomes the proclaimer. Insofar as preaching . . . offers the life of God in Christ, it is Jesus himself who is the preacher."[6]

Evangelism

"For God so loved the world that He gave His only begotten Son, that whoever believes in Him should not perish but have everlasting life" (John 3:16, NKJV). This verse expresses the greatest reality known to the human race.

When a person discovers this truth through the saving grace of God in Christ, it is only natural for him or her to want to tell others. And this our Lord commissions us to do: "Go therefore and make disciples of all the nations, baptizing them in the name of the Father and of the Son and of the Holy Spirit, teaching them to observe all things that I have commanded you; and lo, I am with you always, even to the end of the age" (Matt. 28:19-20, NKJV).

Evangelism is not "politically correct" in some religious and cultural settings. But Christians are not arrogant when they share Jesus Christ, the Bread of Life. We are like one beggar telling another where the bread (Bread) is. Augustine called the bearer of the gospel a little basket in which the bread, the Bread of Life, is laid. Could any Christian find a more noble vocation? Thus, we willingly answer the call to become "ambassadors for Christ, as though God were pleading through us . . . be reconciled to God" (2 Cor. 5:20, NKJV).

About a quarter million new Nazarenes were received into membership from 1992 to 1996, for a net gain of 146,000. Each world region reported good gains. Africa and South America showed phenomenal growth. During that quadrennium, 24,879 Nazarenes in 1,484 Work and Witness teams paid their own expenses to mission fields, where they donated the cumulative equivalent of 812 years of labor!

Nazarenes give generously for world evangelism, placing $197.6 million in the offering plates for missions during the 1992-96 period. There are now 665 Nazarene missionaries at work in 116 countries. Twenty-nine countries have sent their people to Nazarene mission fields.

But evangelism is not just mission work. Nazarenes evangelize through revivals, personal evangelism, lifestyle evangelism, new churches, Sunday Schools, small groups, community and youth programs, and a dozen other methods.

Nurture

"The Lord has given us to each other to strengthen each other's hands."[7] These wise words of John Wesley pinpoint the heart and core of Christian nurture.

Christian nurture is a labor of love, and it drinks of that same spirit that moved Paul to write to the Thessalonians: "So deeply do we care for you that we are determined to share with you not only the gospel of God but also our own selves, because you have become very dear to us" (1 Thess. 2:8, NRSV).

Christian nurture includes everything the church does to teach, promote spiritual growth, and make disciples. It includes faith mentoring, Bible study groups, support groups, family worship, spiritual formation, Christian camping, Sunday School, Christian colleges, and just plain Christian fellowship.

The goal is to bring everyone to "the knowledge of the Son of God, to maturity, to the measure of the full stature of Christ" (Eph. 4:13, NRSV).

Nazarenes conduct many educational enterprises. Strong Sunday Schools have been a Nazarene hallmark around the world. Small-group ministries patterned after John Wesley's classes and bands still flourish. The Nazarene Publishing House is the largest producer of Holiness literature in the world. World Mission Radio and the broadcasting arms of the Communications Division give "Nazarene nurture" an international presence. One nurturing venture that truly characterizes us these days is our colleges, seminaries, universities, and Bible colleges. By 1921 we had 12 institutions of higher learning; now we have 59, educating 26,000 students on their campuses and extension programs with a combined annual budget of about $175 million and assets of about $307 million.[8]

Nazarenes seem to know what John Greenleaf Whittier was talking about when he wrote,

> It need not fear the skeptic's puny hand
> While near the school the church shall stand,
> Nor fear the blinded bigot's rule
> When near the church shall stand the school.[9]

As A. M. Hills, a founder of Olivet Nazarene University, put it, "Spirituality without intellectuality becomes fanaticism, and intellectuality without spirituality becomes infidelity."[10]

Nurture is the very essence of the Wesleyan-Holiness tradition, as this Charles Wesley hymn shows:

> *Help us to help each other, Lord;*
> *Each other's cross to bear.*
> *Let each his friendly aid afford*
> *And feel his brother's care.*
>
> *Help us to build each other up,*
> *Our little stock improve;*
> *Increase our faith, confirm our hope,*
> *And perfect us in love.*[11]

Service

Christian service is not optional. Maxie Dunnam was right: "A spirituality that does not lead to active ministry becomes an indulgent preoccupation with self, and therefore grieves the Holy Spirit and violates the presence of the indwelling Christ."[12] Mother Teresa put it this way: "There is too much talk. . . . Take a broom and clean someone's house. That says enough."[13]

John Wesley declared, "I do not acknowledge him to have one grain of faith who is not continually . . . willing to spend and be spent in doing all good . . . to all men."[14] Phineas F. Bresee wrote, "The evidence of the presence of Jesus in our midst is that we bear the gospel, primarily, to the poor." He added, "I may have faith that moves mountains, and if I lack the great love that stoops to lift men, I am nothing—*no thing.*"

Poverty has reached critical dimensions in our world. But Nazarenes have energetically reclaimed their biblical and Wesleyan heritage to "spend and be spent" for others. Nazarenes gave nearly $9.5 million for compassionate ministries for the poor and oppressed. The denomination operates 100 compassionate ministry centers and has 700 Good Samaritan churches reaching out to persons in all kinds of emergencies.

There are so many avenues and channels for service among us that joining the Nazarenes is a move toward giving your life away in service to Christ and the people for whom He died.

So there you have it—a glimpse of what the Church of the Nazarene believes and practices. If you like what you see, come share the dream.

PART 2

OUR CLOSEST KIN:
THE METHODIST AND HOLINESS CHURCHES

At a Glance

Early Wesleyan Foundations

Historical Roots

John Wesley (1703-91), preacher's kid and Oxford University professor, was the founding father of the Methodist movement. John and his cohorts sought to reform the nation, particularly the church, and to spread scriptural holiness throughout Britain—and beyond. To do this, they created societies, classes, bands, and mentoring pairs to help people in the pursuit of Christian perfection. They also reached out in unprecedented ways to the brutalized masses with food, clothing, health care, education, and the gospel.

Core Beliefs

Early Wesleyanism embraced a theology of grace—prevenient grace, saving grace, sanctifying grace.

The church's aim was the salvation of souls.

Entire sanctification was the engine that drove the movement.

Wesleyanism modeled a conscious choice for the poor and oppressed.

Wesleyans were committed to the church as a community in which Christians helped each other in the pursuit and practice of perfect love.

Wesleyans embraced orthodox Christianity, including a belief in the sufficiency of Scripture to reveal the way of salvation.

Personal religious experience that brings inner assurance of grace (rather than formal religion) marked the early Methodists.

Agreement and Differences

Nazarenes find little to disagree with on early Wesleyan core beliefs. In fact, our founding fathers modeled our own beliefs and practices after Wesley's. Though changing times produce adaptations, Nazarenes still believe it would be difficult to find a more balanced, biblical, and practical starting point from which to carry out the mission to which Christ has called us than the model of those early Wesleyans.

Wesleyanism Today

Though some have taken liberties with the heritage, some 80 denominations worldwide regard Wesley as ecclesiastical ancestor, including the United Methodist Church, The Wesleyan Church, the Free Methodist Church, and the Church of the Nazarene.

**"My heart was strangely warmed. I felt
I did trust in Christ, Christ alone for
salvation, and an assurance was given me
that He had taken away *my* sins,
even *mine*."**

—John Wesley

CHAPTER 3

EARLY WESLEYAN FOUNDATIONS

LIKE MAPLE LEAVES before a cold November wind, England's industrial revolution swept the poor into the cities, leaving them piled in random heaps. Housing conditions were outrageous. Ten persons per room was common. Horse manure polluted unpaved streets, piling 14 feet high beside some London thoroughfares. Typhoid, cholera, dysentery, and smallpox ravaged the population. Some 90 percent of the population were poor, 40 percent desperately so. Starvation was a daily reality, reported in almost every edition of every newspaper. Graveyards kept gaping "poor holes"—large, common graves left open until the daily flow of nameless corpses filled them.

Violent crime was an everyday occurrence. Gambling and gin drinking became the national pastimes. Every sixth building in London was an alehouse, and England was easily the most drunken nation in the world. Sports included boxing, bullbaiting, cockfighting, and hangings. For children, there were the streets or the sweatshops. Only 1 in 25 attended a school of any kind.

Henry Fielding described the London in which he lived: "The poor are a very great burden and ever a nuisance. . . . There are whole families in want of every necessity of life, oppressed with hunger, cold, nakedness and filth and disease. . . . They starve and freeze and rot among themselves . . . steal and beg and rob among their betters."[1]

A letter from John Wesley appeared in the *London Chronicle, Lloyd's Evening Post,* and the *Leeds Mercury*. It read in part:

Why are thousands of people starving? . . . I've seen it with my own eyes in every corner of the land. I have known those who could only afford to eat a little coarse food every other day. I have known one picking up stinking sprats from a dunghill and carrying them home for herself and her children. I have known another gathering the bones which the dogs have left in the streets and making broth of them to prolong a wretched life. Why are so many thousand people in London, in Bristol, in Norwich, in every county from one end of England to the other, utterly destitute of employment?[2]

Workers labored under debilitating conditions. Twelve- to 15-hour days in the coal mines or textile mills were the rule. The miners were desperate. Long hours in the damp bowels of the earth made "rheumatism universal and consumption common."[3] Accidents and poison gas took their lives daily. A newspaper reported, "The catastrophe from foul air [in the mines] becomes more common than ever; yet as we have been requested to take no particular notice of these things, which, in fact could have little good tendency, we drop the farther mentioning of it."[4]

Women worked in coal mines "as beasts of burden and, with chains around their waists, crawled on hands and knees through narrow passages, drawing after them the coal carriages."[5] Workers as young as three were recruited by textile mills, where working conditions rivaled those of the mines.

Enclosure Acts drove the poor off the common lands where for centuries they had gathered firewood and raised their cabbages, chickens, parsnips, and pigs. Now they had no land, garden, or job. A Leeds journalist declared, "The poor are without relief . . . without fuel, without food, and without the lawful means of securing them."[6]

When lawful means of survival are not available, the unlawful will do. A man being executed for participating in two hunger riots was asked by the *London Chronicle* why he did such a thing. He answered, "We did not desire to hear our children weep for bread and [have] none to give them."[7]

The Grand Jury of the King's Bench was asked to consider the swarms of hungry people choking the London streets. Describing them as a "dreadful nuisance" so "burthensome and disgraceful," the Grand Jury recommended enforcing the laws more vigorously, "that we may not be thus troubled with the Poor."[8]

No fewer than 250 offenses were punishable by death. Death sentences were dished out for stealing a sheep, a loaf of bread, a piece of cheese, or trying to pick a pocket. Those committing crimes against the gentry were punished especially harshly. Every Lent and Christmas season, the courts carried out a bloody pageant of death. The trials were the central attraction, but balls, business conferences, and other social events were held during "assize week." Before the trials began, a high-ranking priest from the state church gave a sermon to convicts and the crowd, blessing what the court was about to do. And the courts, week after week, year after year, handed down the same penalty of death to offenders, whether guilty of murder or stealing a simple piece of bread. Thousands of poor "criminals" were deported as indentured servants to Africa, Australia, and America. Others were whipped, burned, and jailed. Death sentences were passed out to children as young as 10 as England hanged up to 500 of her citizens per year.

Enter John Wesley

Into this scene of judicial oppression, official indifference, and dire poverty walked a little man with a Bible under his arm. John Wesley was only 5'6" tall and never weighed over 135 pounds, but the "little giant" led England in a revival of religion that has been called the Methodist Revolution. This Christ-centered campaign lifted the social and spiritual life of the brutalized masses.

John Wesley was born in 1703 to devout parents. His father, Samuel, was an Anglican priest and scholar. His mother, Susanna, was a remarkable woman of learning and devotion. She gave personal religious instruction to her children besides making a successful school of her home, where she taught other children as well. The 25th child of her father, she gave birth to 19 children. John, her 15th child, treasured her counsel.

When John was 17, he went to Oxford University. In 1724 he graduated from that school. In 1726 he became a teacher at Oxford's Lincoln College. He received his master's degree from Oxford in 1727, and in 1728 he was ordained as an Anglican (Church of England) priest. The founder of Methodism remained an Anglican priest all his life.

At Oxford, John and his younger brother, Charles, became involved with a group of earnest students who wanted more than anything else to do God's will every hour of every day. They attracted pejorative labels— "Bible moths," "Methodists," "the Holy Club." "Methodists" was the one that stuck. While others laughed at them, they gave themselves to devotion, study, and daily work with the sick, poor, and imprisoned.

Next, in 1736, Wesley tried his hand at winning the Indians of Georgia to Christ. His ministry to colonists and Native Americans in this American colony proved more a failure than a success. He returned to England in less than two years to resume working with his fellow Methodists in London.

Personal Religion

On May 24, 1738, Wesley's long and painful search for a heartfelt personal relationship with Christ fruitfully ended. He "unwillingly" attended a society meeting where someone was reading aloud Luther's introduction to Romans. As Luther described salvation by faith alone, Wesley felt his heart "strangely warmed." "I felt I did trust in Christ, Christ alone for salvation, and an assurance was given me that he had taken away *my* sins, even *mine,* and saved me from the law of sin and death."[9]

With this new religion of the heart burning inside, Wesley was ready to take his place alongside such colleagues as George Whitefield in spearheading a revival that changed England and much of the world.

Whitefield and Wesley, among others, took their message to the people by preaching in the fields and streets. Thousands turned out to hear them. Souls who were renewed under his preaching were organized by Wesley into "societies," "classes," "bands," and mentoring pairs for the nurture of personal religion and the pursuit of Christian perfection.

To date, no one has improved on Wesley's pastoral theology and scheme of spiritual formation. Besides attending the principal services of the Church of England, the new Methodists met twice weekly in "societies" for instruction and preaching. Each society member was required to join a "class" of 12 persons who met weekly for mutual support and religious instruction. Those who hungered for a still deeper walk with God were invited, after spiritual examination, to join a "band." This was a group of 4 to 6 persons of the same gender who weekly shared their spiritual journey "without reserve and without disguise." Each meeting began by hearing any spiritual failures that members had encountered that week. Prayer and restoration followed. Next, persons shared the temptations they had encountered, and the strategies and devotions that had delivered them. Wesley felt that Methodism did its best work in the bands.

Wesley also arranged for hundreds of Methodists to be associated in mentoring pairs or "twin soul" pairs. Spiritual fathers and mothers were directed to mentor specific new Christians. Twin soul pairs were Christians of like faith paired off as spiritual friends and mutual spiritual guides (not spiritual directors). All this—societies, classes, bands, mentoring pairs, and twin souls—Wesley called "Christian Conference." It conserved the fruits of revival, produced stronger Christians, provided loving accountability among believers, created an arena for sanctifying grace to be sought and experienced, and produced deep mutual devotion and lifelong friendships. Wesley's system of family religion was also a form of Christian Conference that must be taken seriously.[10]

Wesley told Frances Godfrey, "It is a blessed thing to have fellow travellers to the New Jerusalem. If you do not find any, you must make them, for none can travel this road alone."[11] To William Holland, Mr. Wesley wrote, "The Lord has given us to each other . . . that we may strengthen each other's hands in Him."[12] Nothing more astutely sums up the Methodist commitment to Christian Conference.

A cadre of itinerant preachers or helpers, many lay preachers, and an army of class leaders managed this system of Christian nurture. Wesley's Methodism soon became the most efficient organization or "connexion" in all England. George Whitefield moved from one mass revival meeting to another. Looking back late in his career, he mourned, "Brother Wesley acted wisely. The souls that were awakened under his ministry, he joined in class, and thus preserved the fruits of his labor. This I neglected, and my people are a rope of sand."[13]

Social Responsibility

John Wesley and his Methodists modeled for the world a near-perfect marriage of personal religion and social responsibility. Perhaps no other group has ever lived out the vows of this marriage better. It was not enough for early Wesleyans to attend society, class, band, prayer, and mentoring pair meetings in an all-out pursuit of Christian perfection. No, for them Christian service was just as much a spiritual discipline as prayer and fasting.

Wesley declared, "Nor do we acknowledge him to have one grain of faith . . . who is not willing to 'spend and be spent' in doing all good, as he has opportunity, to all men."[14] True Christianity brings with it, Wesley believed, "a hunger and thirsting to do good of every possible kind." He called himself God's steward for the poor. "Join hands with God, to make a poor man live!" was a frequent plea.[15] Every class and band meeting included an offering for the poor. The goal was "to deal your bread to the hungry, and cover the naked with a garment, . . . and put them [our poor] in a way of supplying their own wants for the time to come."[16]

Wesley and his people engaged in all sorts of ministries, including the following:

1. Schools of many kinds—literacy schools, Sunday Schools, adult education schools, ministerial schools, day schools, residential schools.

2. Sick ministries. London was divided into districts, and Methodists were assigned to visit each sick person at least three times a week, checking on the state of his or her soul and health.

3. Medical care. John Wesley established the first free medical clinic in England in 1748.

4. Food and clothing distribution, particularly in London and Bristol.

5. Ministry to unwed or destitute mothers. The Lying In Hospital in London provided prenatal and postnatal care, religious instruction, and vocational training for about 300 women per year.

6. The Stranger's Friend Society. This was a charity created by Methodists for non-Methodists. It soon spread throughout the land, and even the king and queen contributed to it.

7. The Christian Community ministered to the "paupers and vagabonds" in the London workhouses.

8. A widows' home in London.

9. An orphanage in New Castle.

10. Unemployment relief—jobs for out-of-work Methodists—was provided. The project failed, but the attempt was made.

11. Small business loan fund. Methodists who wanted to go into business for themselves could get a loan from a Methodist fund to help them launch it.

12. Prison ministries. In order to join the Bristol Methodist society, one had to pledge to do prison work. Newgate Prison in Bristol was a "region of horror . . . so great was the filth, the stench, the misery, and wickedness which shocked all who had a spark of humanity left."[17] Soon the Wesleyans got a Methodist appointed as warden. The prison was reformed, and the whole kingdom was invited by Wesley to come and see how a prison should be run in a Christian country. Charles Wesley, the hymn writer, was one of the tireless workers who helped make this happen.

In addition to the reform and purification the early Wesleyans urged in public, they privately devoted themselves to heart purity, to Christian perfection, and to holiness of heart. Wesley called sanctifying grace "the medicine of life, the never failing remedy for all the evils of a disordered world, for all the miseries and vices of men."[18]

The Essence of Methodism

John Wesley created a theology for his times. His every doctrinal innovation can be traced not only to the Scriptures and Christian creeds but also to distinct needs of the times. His teaching against predestination and for free grace, for example, taught his brutalized masses to hope. Their poverty, ignorance, and suffering, far from being what God had planned for them, was to be seen as a contradiction to God's will for them. When Wesley began to teach human freedom and equality, he was attacked by politicians and Anglican clergy for conspiring against divine Providence by changing the estate of the poor.

Wesley's theological method was simple: study the needs of the times, then examine all the resources of the Christian faith, and bring resources and needs together. After Wesley, others would speak of his method in terms of the Wesleyan quadrilateral, a device by which ideas and doctrines are tested by Scripture (first of all), reason (does it make sense?), tradition (what has the Church done and said about this matter in the past?), and experience (is the idea under discussion consistent with the religious experience of God's people?).

The core beliefs of early Methodism are simple.

1. Salvation is the central aim. Whatever acts of piety and mercy the Wesleyans gave themselves to, the overarching aim was the salvation of souls. The Methodists took sin seriously. Something had gone wrong with the human enterprise. The human heart, as Albert Outler has said, is a tinderbox of sin. No list of legalisms, no stack of self-help psychology books could cure it.

What is salvation? Wesley said, "By salvation I mean, not barely, according to the vulgar notion, deliverance from hell, or going to heaven; but a present deliverance from sin, a restoration of the soul to its primitive health, its original purity; a recovery of the divine nature; the renewal of our souls after the image of God, in righteousness and true holiness, in justice, mercy, and truth."[19] Early Wesleyans wanted a personal knowledge of Christ as Savior.

2. Sanctification is both the organizing principle and the most distinctive contribution of Wesleyan spiritual theology. No doctrine is more characteristic of early Methodism. It is the capstone of all of Wesley's paradigms for spiritual formation. It flies in the face of traditional Protestant thought, which declares humanity to be so sinful that we will never get over our depravity in this life. Wesley boldly preached that the believer's heart can be cleansed from all sin and filled with divine love. To Lawrence Coughlan, Wesley wrote that holiness was "the love of God and our neighbour; the image of God stamped on the heart . . . the mind that was in Christ, enabling us to walk as Christ also walked . . . that deep communion with the Father and the Son, whereby they are enabled to give Him their whole heart, to love every man as their own soul."[20]

This was a perfection of heart and intentions, but certainly not of performance. A thousand infirmities that go with being members of a fallen race that bears the brunt of centuries of sin will plague our best efforts. But as Wesley wrote to Dorothy Furly, "I want you to be all love. This is the perfection I believe and teach."[21] To young theologian Joseph Benson, Wesley defined full salvation as "an entire deliverance from [willful] sin, a recovery of the whole image of God, the loving God with all our heart, soul, and strength."[22]

3. **Wesleyanism is anchored in grace.** Salvation by grace alone is so foundational to Wesleyanism that Henry Bett declared, "From the days of Wesley to the present, no Methodist has ever dreamed of grounding the forgiveness of sins on anything but the free grace of God and the redemptive work of Christ."[23] The Wesleyan system is a progression of grace: atoning grace, prevenient grace, justifying (saving) grace, sanctifying grace, perfecting grace, and glorifying grace. Deeds of piety and service are required, but only God's grace saves.

4. **Wesleyanism rests in the sufficiency of Holy Scripture.** "O give me that book! At any price give me the book of God!" cried John Wesley. "I have it: here is knowledge enough for me. Let me be *homo unis libri* [a man of one book]."[24] For those early Wesleyans, the Bible was the first and final authority. Yet the Methodist approach to Scripture is wide-scoped, not fundamentalistic. It focuses on biblical principles and does not take Bible passages out of context. The rigid, legalistic debate on inerrancy did not spring from Methodist soil. Methodists believe that Scripture is sufficient to reveal to us the way of salvation. True Wesleyans take the Bible too seriously to chop it up into proof texts.

5. **Wesleyanism embraces a catholic spirit.** The catholic spirit of early Methodism does not mean that it was like the Roman Catholic Church. Rather, John Wesley was convinced that what believers had in common through Christ was more important than their denominational differences. Provincialism and sectarianism are foreign to the Wesleyan spirit. Wesley declared that "God has given no right to any . . . to lord it over the conscience of his brethren."[25] He pled, rather, "Though we cannot think alike, may we not love alike? May we not be of one heart, though we are not of one opinion?"[26] He announced, "If thine heart is as my heart, if thou lovest God and all mankind, I ask no more: give me thine hand."[27]

6. **Wesleyanism is Christ-centered.** Of Wesley, Albert Outler wrote, "In a hundred different ways, on thousands of different occasions, decade after five decades, his message was Jesus Christ and Him crucified—*Christus crucifixus, Christus redemptor, Christus Victor.*"[28]

7. **The genius of early Methodism was creative synthesis.** Wesley was committed to the synthetic method. In working out theology, doctrine, polity, or educational philosophy, he consulted a wide variety of sources and resources. Governed by the theological norms of the "quadrilateral" (Revelation, reason, tradition, experience), he braided new ropes to rescue the perishing. He was unafraid to "plunder the Egyptians" of medicine, literature, secular philosophy, or business. For example, where in the Bible would Wesley learn how to establish a credit union or loan fund to help Methodists start their own businesses? He turned to both secular and religious educators to come up with a way to run the Foundery and Kingswood schools. Governed by the quadrilateral whenever a one-sided traditionalism, rationalism, experimentalism, or biblicism threatened, "there was from the beginning a built-in Wesleyan resistance to each of these approaches pursued in isolation."[29]

8. **Early Methodism emphasized vital religious experience.** "I want that faith which none can have without knowing that he hath it," prayed the young Wesley.[30] Empty formal religion does not satisfy the Wesleyan quest for the religion of the heart. Wesley declared, "He wants a religion of a nobler kind, a religion higher and deeper than this. He can no more feed on this poor, shallow, formal thing than he can 'fill his belly with the east wind.'"[31]

9. **Wesleyanism accents the church as a community of faith.** Wesley believed that "social holiness" was genuine and essential to faith. Therefore, Methodism prized public preaching, corporate worship, and small-group ministries. The principles of Christian fellowship demonstrated in the societies, classes, bands, mentoring pairs, and love feast characterize genuine Wesleyanism.

10. **Wesleyanism contains a magnetic attraction to the poor and oppressed.** It renounces "private piety that clings to Jesus and ignores the human agonies of this world."[32] Just as Jesus validated His messianic credentials by citing His ministry to the blind, the lame, the lepers, the deaf, and the poor, Wesleyanism validates itself by a conscious choice for the poor and oppressed.

The early Methodists set high benchmarks for the 80 churches and denominations that today describe themselves as belonging to the Wesleyan tradition.

AT A GLANCE

AMERICAN METHODISTS

Historical Roots

Methodism came to America in the 1760s. Barbara Heck, an Irish immigrant, helped start the first Methodist society in America in 1768. The Christmas Conference of 1784 in Baltimore created the Methodist Episcopal Church. Francis Asbury, one of Wesley's missionaries, became its strongest leader. African-American Methodism and German Methodism also helped write the Wesleyan story in America.

Core Beliefs

The core beliefs of Methodism include orthodox Protestant theology, including beliefs in the triune God; Christ as Savior; justification by faith; sacraments of baptism and the Lord's Supper; prevenient, saving, and sanctifying grace; and the sufficiency of Scripture. The *Discipline* also provides for "exploratory" theologizing, which has engaged the denomination in Black, feminist, liberation, and process theologies.

Agreement and Differences

The Nazarenes and today's Methodists are in harmony on basic Protestant orthodoxy and Arminian views. Differences come at the scope of theological teaching approved by the Methodists. Theologians and pastors are free to pursue "exploratory" theologies. Nazarenes by design stick primarily to the traditional Wesleyan teachings. In spite of the orthodox statements in the *Discipline*, the breadth of what a Methodist can teach puzzles some Nazarenes.

Nazarenes and Methodists tend to differ on our cardinal doctrine—sanctification. Methodists commonly promote sanctification as process. Nazarenes and the American Holiness Movement prefer Wesley's teachings that entire sanctification has both processive and instantaneous aspects. Methodists commonly think of conversion in terms of Christian nurture. Nazarenes know conversion as an instantaneous experience.

American Methodists Today

The United Methodist Church is the second largest Protestant denomination in America. Add three African-American Methodist groups, and there are 14 million Methodists in America.

> **Q. What may we reasonably believe to be God's design in raising up the Methodist preachers?**
> **A. To reform the Continent, and to spread scriptural Holiness over these Lands.**
>
> —First *Discipline* of the Methodist Episcopal Church

CHAPTER 4

AMERICAN METHODISTS

THE UNITED METHODIST cross-and-flame logo is perhaps the best-recognized denominational symbol in America. It combines symbols of Christ and the Holy Spirit. Its two tongues of fiery red flame, united at the bottom, also symbolize the 1968 union of the Methodist and Evangelical United Brethren Churches.

Methodists are a large proportion of worshiping Americans. The United Methodist Church, with over 8.5 million U.S. members, is the second largest Protestant denomination in North America and has another 1 million members in other countries. Three predominantly African-American Methodist churches total another 5.5 million members in the United States.

American Methodism was the product of British Methodism's missionary impulse. Planted in the 1760s, Methodism grew to be the largest American denomination by 1850. They did so because they were not paralyzed by the challenge of competing within a religious environment dominated by Calvinism. At the same time, they became the most American church, exposed fully to the stresses of national life. Racism and ethnicity exacted their price, as did democratization. Three traditions developed: a central one embodied by the Methodist Episcopal Church, and distinctly African and German forms of Methodism.

Francis Asbury

The first American Methodists were immigrants like Barbara Heck (a native of Limerick, Ireland) who brought their Methodist faith with them. In 1768 Heck helped organize the first Methodist society in America at New York City.[1]

John Wesley sent lay preachers to lead these societies and organize new ones. Earnest but conservative, those preachers returned to England when the American Revolution came. There was one exception: Francis Asbury (1745—1816) alone adapted to the American spirit and remained to supervise the Methodist enterprise. Despite the turmoil of war, Methodism sank deep roots into American culture during the Revolution. The preachers were sufficiently strong as a body to organize the first Methodist denomination in the world in 1784.

Why did the Americans leave Wesley's Church of England and strike out on their own? The factors included

• the sacramental crisis
• an urgency to evangelize the American people
• their acceptance of the daunting challenges that America's physical and social environment posed

The Church of England's failure to place a bishop in America before or after the Revolution provoked the sacramental crisis. With no bishop, it was impossible under Anglican polity to ordain priests in the New World. The resulting shortage of priests meant infrequent baptisms, Communion, and preaching.

Wesley felt he could not wait for his church to act. In 1784 he authorized Thomas Coke (1747—1814), an Anglican priest like himself, as one of two general superintendents of the American Methodists. Wesley also ordained several lay preachers into the ministry. This was entirely irregular by Anglican standards. Only bishops could ordain, but Wesley felt that "emergency ministers" were needed. Coke was authorized to ordain Francis Asbury, whom Wesley appointed as the other general superintendent.

Asbury traveled by horse and carriage the length of the new nation and a full third of its breadth. Sanctified Methodist Richard Whatcoat was elected bishop in 1801 to assist him. Whatcoat was succeeded by William McKendree, the first American-born bishop and a rugged frontier revivalist who commanded the preachers' respect. Under Asbury, Whatcoat, and McKendree, Methodism's strategy for evangelizing North America took shape.

"To Reform the Nation"

Methodists succeeded in the 19th century for several reasons. Among them:

• the circuit rider
• the class meeting and class leader
• the camp meeting revival

- the message
- the appointive system in which ministers were assigned by the bishop

America was largely a frontier society. The Methodist minister traveled a circuit that could have 20 or more preaching points. Bishops deployed the preachers in ways that covered large territories. This also forced the church to rely on strong lay leaders in the interim between pastoral visits. The physical demands were horrendous, and many were worn-out preachers by middle age. Locally, Methodists were organized into classes under spiritual leaders. Preaching and Communion services were held when the ordained minister visited, but some class leaders were also licensed local preachers.

The camp meeting was an effective Methodist tool. Large groups gathered, sometimes by the thousands, with simultaneous preaching in different parts of the camp. Asbury always estimated by hundreds the number who were converted, sanctified, and took Communion at these gatherings.

Today it is common to see large Methodist churches in urban areas. But Methodism has always been strongly rural. By following the frontier and ministering to the homesteaders, the Methodists spread more evenly across America than any other group.

While Asbury and his successors carried on, German Americans formed two separate Methodistic groups, which eventually combined in the Evangelical United Brethren Church. In turn, it merged with the Methodist Church, creating the United Methodist Church.

African Methodism

Black Methodists in Philadelphia and other major American cities typically were discriminated against by White Methodists. Segregated seating and Communion practices and other prejudices led to the rise of the African Methodist Episcopal Church in 1816. Richard Allen (1760—1831), a former slave, was its first bishop. Its *Discipline*, Articles of Religion, and General Rules were nearly identical to the M.E. Church's. A similar denomination took shape in New York City in 1820. James Varick was the first general superintendent of the African Methodist Episcopal Zion Church. Like the A.M.E. Church, the A.M.E. Zion Church actively opposed slavery, and its members included Frederick Douglass, Sojourner Truth, and Harriet Tubman. A third expression of Black Methodism originated in the South after the Civil War: the Colored Methodist Episcopal Church was created in 1870. In 1954, its name changed to the Christian Methodist Episcopal Church. Today, the A.M.E. Church's membership is 3.5 million, the A.M.E. Zion Church has over 1.2 million members, and the C.M.E. Church's membership is 718,000.[2]

United Methodist Theology

What does today's United Methodist Church teach? The *Discipline* (1996) lists these basic theological affirmations:
- faith in the mystery of salvation in and through Jesus Christ
- belief that God's redemptive love is realized in human life by the activity of the Holy Spirit in personal experience and in the community of believers
- the essential oneness of Christ's Church
- belief that the United Methodist Church is part of Christ's universal Church "when by adoration, proclamation, and service we become conformed to Christ"
- scriptural authority in matters of faith
- justification by grace through faith
- the sober realization that the church is in need of continual reformation and renewal
- understanding God's reign as both present and future[3]

Each aspect ties the United Methodist witness to the Church Universal. But a further summary notes "distinctive Wesleyan emphases":
- prevenient grace
- justification by grace
- assurance of present salvation
- sanctification and perfection, described primarily as a process of growth in grace
- faith as "the only response essential to salvation" yet dead without works of mercy
- Christian fellowship as essential both for the nurture and mission of the body of Christ[4]

The *Discipline* contains two different creeds: the Twenty-five Articles of the Methodist Episcopal Church (1784) and the Confession of Faith of the Evangelical United Brethren Church. Both reflect basic Protestant orthodoxy. The article on "Sanctification and Christian Perfection" from the Evangelical United Brethren Church Confession affirms in part:
- Entire sanctification is a state of perfect love, righteousness and true holiness which every regenerate believer may obtain.
- Through faith in Jesus Christ this gracious gift may be received in this life both gradually and instantaneously, and should be sought by every child of God.[5]

A section of the *Discipline* titled "Our Theological Task" emphasizes that the church has a continuing theological vocation. It states that the church "encourages serious reflection across the theological spectrum. . . .

We are called to identify the needs both of individuals and of society and to address those needs out of the resources of Christian faith. . . . Theology serves the Church by interpreting the world's needs and challenges to the Church and by interpreting the gospel to the world."[6] Thus, Methodists believe that "exploratory theologies"—feminist theology, liberation theology, Black theology, process theology, and other schools of thought—assist them in reaching out to the contemporary world.

A set of United Methodist social principles are included in the *Discipline*. They establish a theological framework for Christian moral thinking in four broad areas: the natural world, the compassionate community, society, and economics.

A final section titled "The Ministry of All Christians" calls the church "the people of God" and teaches that all Christians are ministers, that baptism marks one's entry into the ministry of the church, and that "the impulse to minister always moves one beyond the congregation toward the whole human community." A belief in lay ministry still permeates United Methodist thought as it did earlier on the frontier.

Within this framework of the ministry of all Christians, two types of full-time ministers are ordained: deacons and elders.[7]

United Methodists also practice inclusiveness. Women and racial/ethnic minorities are always well represented at public gatherings of the church.

Nazarenes and Methodists

What do we owe the United Methodist Church? More, frankly, than we owe to any other denomination:

- our quadrennial General Assembly
- our *Manual*, patterned originally after the *Discipline*
- our system of districts and district superintendents
- our general superintendency
- our basic theology
- our ordination practices
- the majority of our major founders
- such garden-variety characteristics as district ownership of local church property

Early Nazarene theologian A. M. Hills claimed that "the Church of the Nazarene is the fairest flower that has ever bloomed in the Methodist garden, the most promising ecclesiastical daughter the prolific Mother Methodism has ever given to the world."[8] General Superintendent E. F. Walker insisted: "Scratch a real Nazarene, and you will touch an original Methodist; skin a genuine Methodist, and behold a Nazarene."[9] Hills and Walker were former ministers in Presbyterian and Congregational churches. Despite that fact (or perhaps because of it), they understood the underlying Methodist identity of their new church.

Hills's essay, published for the Church of the Nazarene's 25th anniversary, cited Nazarene continuity with Methodism in six primary areas: pioneer leadership (he mentions Asbury and Bresee), soul winning, missionary endeavor, theological scholarship, spiritual inheritance, and education for a Christian culture.

What differences, then, separate the two denominations? What makes the Church of the Nazarene distinctive and different? First, Nazarenes are distinctly Evangelical and embrace a traditional Wesleyanism. Official United Methodist doctrine expresses orthodox theology, but the range of beliefs among the church's theologians, pastors, and members is much more diverse than the *Discipline* indicates. United Methodists have been so ecumenical and broad-minded that in some times and places they have embraced the radically ultraliberal, and in other times and places the reactionary conservative.

This tolerance for many theologies discourages many traditional Wesleyans within the United Methodist Church. Nevertheless, traditional United Methodist Wesleyans maintain a vigorous camp meeting tradition and support Asbury College, Asbury Theological Seminary, and Taylor University. Their influence is felt in the Christian Holiness Partnership and the Wesleyan Theological Society. Their contribution to the Wesleyan-Holiness tradition's vitality is substantial when one considers that Asbury Theological Seminary trains more ministers than the next three largest Wesleyan-Holiness seminaries combined. United Methodists who reflect the Wesleyan-Holiness identity exist, then, in a theologically pluralistic church. By contrast, the Church of the Nazarene maintains a traditional Wesleyan focus.

This leads to another major difference: the Church of the Nazarene's founders created a believers' church. It was set against a mainstream Methodism that they believed had been seduced by American culture. For instance, Nazarene rejection of secret oath-bound societies reflected their belief that the Methodists who belonged to such groups were allowing other loyalties to compete with their loyalty to fellow believers in Christ. The early Nazarene passion to take the gospel to the poor reflected a similar disenchantment with a church they believed was too seduced by rising middle-class prosperity.

The Nazarene founders also were revolutionaries who made all clergy and lay offices in the church open to women. Methodist women still struggled for laity rights, and full clergy rights lay another half century down the road. But Nazarenes simply went ahead and did it. That issue no longer divides us today, and United Methodists have a significantly higher percentage of women pastors. In addition, they have female district superintendents and bishops.

Another difference lies in the basic understanding of how a person typically becomes a Christian. Nazarenes emphasize Christian conversion, both among their own youth and in their outreach to unchurched people. United Methodists, on the other hand, largely emphasize Christian nurture as the primary way of coming to Christ. Altar calls are largely unknown in the United Methodist churches around large urban areas, whereas Nazarene pastors periodically sense a need to preach in a fashion that calls people to a decision.

There is also a corresponding difference in the basic stance on sanctification. Many United Methodists take sanctification very seriously but regard John Wesley's particular theology of holiness, and its possibility of entire sanctification, as an oddity, just as the Calvinists of Wesley's day did. Wesley emphasized three phases of sanctification: initial sanctification (regeneration, the new birth), progressive sanctification (before and after entire sanctification), and entire sanctification (the moment perfect love expels the tendency toward sin). Most United Methodists affirm progressive sanctification only.

Methodism is a worldwide family of churches connected to us by historical ties. The World Methodist Council's member churches include the United Methodist, African Methodist Episcopal, African Methodist Episcopal Zion, and Christian Methodist Episcopal churches. The Free Methodist Church and The Wesleyan Church, the two denominations in the world most nearly like our own, also belong to this council. The World Methodist Council's official handbook includes information about the Church of the Nazarene and other nonmember churches that "have a distinctive Methodist tradition and emphasis." It also includes our worldwide statistics in its studies, showing Methodist penetration country by country. Methodism does not account fully for our identity, but it accounts for much of it. The Methodist story through the 1890s, with its moments of tragedy and grace, is also our story. And the pages of history we and our children write will be further chronicles in the story of Wesley's heirs.

AT A GLANCE

OUR SISTER DENOMINATIONS:
THE HOLINESS CHURCHES

Historical Background

The 19th-century Holiness Movement that swept America brought forth a number of new churches that took as their mission the heralding of the gospel of entire sanctification. Most of them sprang directly from Wesleyan roots, including the Wesleyan Methodist Church, Pilgrim Holiness Church, Free Methodist Church, Church of Christ (Holiness), and, of course, the Church of the Nazarene.

The Church of God (Anderson) and the Church of God (Holiness) also shared the Wesleyan heritage but blended it with a radical doctrine of the church. The Evangelical Friends married Wesleyan doctrine with their Quaker heritage. The Salvation Army was born in England and spread to North America with its message of conversion, entire sanctification, and compassion for the poor.

Core Beliefs and Family Differences

The core beliefs of the churches treated in this chapter include the traditional doctrines of the Trinity, inspiration of Scripture, and salvation by grace through faith in Jesus Christ. For the most part, they are Arminian in theology and Wesleyan in doctrine. They all embrace the key doctrine of sanctification.

Some "family differences" include the rejection of sacraments by The Salvation Army and the Evangelical Friends, opposition to denominational organization and to creeds by the Church of God (Anderson), and the Keswickian sanctification teachings and mild Calvinism of the Christian and Missionary Alliance.

Wesleyan-Holiness Churches Today

The churches treated in this chapter report a constituency of about 4 million. Add to that 1.2 million Nazarenes and the membership of a dozen smaller Wesleyan-Holiness denominations not discussed in this chapter, and you have a sizable army of like-minded Christians.

The Wesleyan Church and the Church of the Nazarene have been the primary groups to gather up the fragmented Wesleyan-Holiness world in the 20th century.

CHAPTER 5

OUR SISTER DENOMINATIONS: THE HOLINESS CHURCHES

THE SEVERAL DOZEN Holiness churches in North America fall into four groups. Those most closely related to the Church of the Nazarene share our Methodist roots and our Evangelical Wesleyan-Holiness theology. The major ones are The Wesleyan Church, Free Methodist Church, The Salvation Army, and Church of God (Anderson, Indiana). The Church of God (Holiness), Church of Christ (Holiness), and Bible Missionary Church are smaller churches that also merit attention.

Another group of churches have non-Methodist origins. Influenced by the 19th-century Holiness revival, they incorporated Wesleyan holiness into their doctrine and Methodist revivalism into their practice, yet they retain key aspects of their original tradition. Major churches in this tier are the Brethren in Christ and Evangelical Friends International.

A third tier is composed of churches that teach entire sanctification as a second work of grace and also embrace 20th-century Pentecostalism. These are discussed in a later chapter.

The fourth tier has one representative, the Christian and Missionary Alliance, which teaches a second work of grace but not according to the Wesleyan-Holiness view. It represents the Keswick-Holiness tradition. Nevertheless, it is similar to Wesleyan-Holiness churches.

Wesleyan-Holiness Relationships

Wesleyan-Holiness churches interact through two primary fellowships. Christian Holiness Partnership began in 1867 as the National Camp Meeting Association for the Promotion of Holiness, better known as the National (and later Christian) Holiness Association. The oldest Holiness association in the world, it once inspired scores of state, county, and local organizations. Methodists tightly controlled it at first, but today its members include the larger Wesleyan-Holiness bodies in North America, several smaller ones, and many evangelical United Methodists. Early Nazarene leaders Phineas Bresee and C. W. Ruth served the National Holiness Association in key positions. One of its key auxiliaries is the Wesleyan Theological Society, founded in 1965. The International Wesleyan-Holiness Women Clergy Conference, which meets every two years, is linked to the Christian Holiness Partnership. The Interchurch Holiness Convention (IHC) was created in the 1950s to serve the conservative North American Holiness Movement. IHC-related groups are committed to the patterns of revivalism that flourished in the early 20th-century Holiness Movement and are culturally conservative.

The Wesleyan Church

The Wesleyan Church enshrines a paradox. It is both the oldest and the youngest of the major Wesleyan-Holiness churches. It was produced by the merger of the Wesleyan Methodist and Pilgrim Holiness denominations in 1968. Of course, each parent body had an older history.

The Wesleyan Methodist Connection began in 1843 when Orange Scott, Luther Lee, and other foes of slavery withdrew from the Methodist Episcopal Church, whose bishops had stifled internal debate over the abolition issue. The Wesleyan Methodists stood for two principles: the abolition of slavery and a church without bishops. Many Wesleyan Methodists were also committed to women's rights.

Orange Scott soon died. After the Civil War, Lee and other surviving founders returned to the Methodist Episcopal Church, which was mounting a major program to educate and assist newly freed slaves. Adam Crooks, however, opposed the reunion movement. In the 1870s he helped the remaining Wesleyan Methodists find a new sense of purpose by leading them to identify more closely with the national Holiness revival.

The Pilgrim Holiness Church was one of the bodies that emerged from that revival. It began as the International Holiness Union and Prayer League, a fellowship founded in 1897 by Martin Wells Knapp (Methodist), Seth Rees (Quaker), and C. W. Ruth (Holiness Christian Church). In 1901 Knapp died, and C. W. Ruth joined the Nazarenes. Rees withdrew over a dispute with Mrs. Knapp in 1905. George Culp, a man of Fundamentalist bent, became the key leader as the group evolved slowly into a denomination known by 1913 as the International Apostolic Holiness Church (IAHC).

Like the Church of the Nazarene, the IAHC gathered many small independent works. Some had Nazarene links, like the Holiness Christian Church and the People's Mission Church in Colorado. The most memorable link was Seth Rees. His brief ministry among Southern California Nazarenes involved a stormy relationship with several men from Bresee's inner circle. In 1917 Rees's large congregation in Pasadena was disorganized by the district superintendent in a drastic attempt to "save" the district. Rees had many Nazarene supporters but did not appeal this decision to the General Assembly. Instead, he formed the Pilgrim Church with about 400 former Nazarenes. In 1922 the Pilgrim Church united with the IAHC, adding Rees's 457 members to a church membership of around 13,000.[1] This brought Rees back into fellowship with a group he had cofounded a quarter century before. The Pilgrim Holiness Church name was adopted at this time, and Rees later was its general superintendent.

The Wesleyan Methodist/Pilgrim Holiness merger in 1968 was a further consolidation. The Wesleyan Church and the Church of the Nazarene have been the primary groups to gather up the fragmented Wesleyan-Holiness world in the 20th century. The Wesleyan Church's educational institutions include Houghton College in Houghton, New York, and Indiana Wesleyan University in Marion, Indiana. The church has 171,000 members in North America and a total constituency of over 300,000.[2]

The Free Methodist Church of North America

Benjamin Titus Roberts founded the Free Methodist Church in 1860. As a Methodist pastor in western New York, Roberts was committed to the doctrine of Christian perfection. He voiced active opposition to growing doctrinal laxity, to slavery, and to Freemasonry's growth among laity and clergy. But his chief concern was to include the poor in the church's life. He spoke against pew rentals, a common method in those days of raising money for local churches, which gave preference to the rich and discriminated against the poor. Roberts tried to persuade one of his congregations to become a "free church." When that failed, he tried enlisting their help to plant one elsewhere in the city.

Roberts established two "free churches" in Buffalo. Other Methodists had established independent "free churches" in the Midwest. In 1860 they joined forces to form the Free Methodist Church. Roberts was elected as its first general superintendent.

Roberts strongly advocated the ordination of women and aligned himself with the laboring class in their conflict with industrialists. His strong witness to entire sanctification was not incidental to his social views. He believed that perfect love had personal and social dimensions and that the gospel should be preached especially to the poor.

After Roberts's death, the term "general superintendent" was replaced by "bishop." Like the Wesleyan Methodist Church, Free Methodism has been centered largely in the Northeast and the upper Midwestern United States. Free Methodists operate several liberal arts institutions, including Seattle Pacific University. The denomination has an inclusive membership of over 80,000 in the United States and Canada.[3]

The Salvation Army

The Salvation Army began in the slums of London in 1865. Originally named the Christian Mission, its focus was the conversion of sinners and the entire sanctification of believers. Many features considered unnecessary to this end—such as the sacraments—were discarded. Its founders, William and Catherine Booth, reorganized it in 1878 as The Salvation Army and gave it a military structure. Ministers were "commissioned" as "officers" and given military type rank instead of being ordained. Lay members were called "soldiers." Their commitment to ministry among the poor resulted in an increasingly strong social ministry to complement its evangelistic one.

George Railton brought the movement to America in 1890. Corps (churches) were established in New York City, St. Louis, and other urban areas. Three of the Booths' children led the American work, including Evangeline Booth. She headed the work in Canada (1896—1904) and the United States (1904-34) before becoming The Salvation Army's fourth "general" and leading the worldwide movement (1934-39). The Salvation Army has nearly 171,000 full members in the United States and Canada. Its North American membership (including children and associate members) is nearly 550,000.[4]

Church of God (Anderson, Indiana)

Another early Holiness church was related less closely to Methodism. The Church of God Reformation movement originated through Daniel Sidney Warner's ministry. Warner opposed all denominations as evil. He regarded entire sanctification as a source of spiritual power and unity that would make nonsectarian Christianity a triumphant reality. In 1881 he founded the *Gospel Trumpet* to promote his views regarding the restoration of "true Christianity." The Church of God Reformation movement was promoted by bands of itinerant gospel workers who preached on street corners, ministered in slums, and held church revivals.

After Warner's death, Church of God leaders backed away from his claim that the movement was "the true Church" and began cooperating with other Holiness bodies. Today it is active in the Christian Holiness Partnership and the National Association of Evangelicals. It remains congregational in government and has no formal creed. An annual camp meeting in Anderson, Indiana, draws around 20,000 people and serves as the church's convention.

The national offices are also located in Anderson, together with a college (Anderson University) and seminary (Anderson School of Theology). Its "Christian Brotherhood Hour" radio broadcast reaches around the world. Renowned preacher and homiletics teacher James Earl Massey is a minister in the church. Its North American constituency is over 228,000, with its worldwide constituency at nearly a half million.[5]

Church of God (Holiness)

Others followed the Anderson folks down a sectarian path, including the Church of God (Holiness), which stemmed from the Southwestern Holiness Association, centered in Missouri and Kansas. The association was gripped by strong antidenomination fervor in 1882. Under A. M. Kiergan's influence, an independent congregation was organized in Centralia, Missouri, in 1883. Kiergan's message of restoring the "true gospel" (holiness) and "true church order" (radical congregationalism) inspired other Churches of God to spring up in the area. John P. Brooks of Illinois joined the Church of God (Holiness) in 1886 and six years later set forth a detailed and systematic argument for the union of "true holiness" and congregationalism in his book *The Divine Church*.[6] Today the Church of God (Holiness) perpetuates the emphases of its founders and regards its congregational government as scripturally prescribed. Its headquarters are in Overland Park, Kansas. Its estimated membership is under 4,000.

Church of Christ (Holiness) U.S.A.

Charles Price Jones and C. H. Mason were among the Black Southerners expelled from Baptist circles in the late 1890s for preaching Wesleyan doctrine. Jones led in organizing the Churches of God in Christ, but dissension fell upon the group after Mason accepted tongues-speaking Pentecostalism in 1907. Mason and his Pentecostal followers were expelled. Jones reorganized the work under the name "Church of Christ (Holiness)." Jones was a gifted gospel songwriter whose contributions include "Deeper, Deeper" and "I Would Not Be Denied." Jackson, Mississippi, is the headquarters of the denomination, which supports a college there. It reported over 9,000 members in 1965.[7]

Bible Missionary Church

The Bible Missionary Church was organized by conservatives who left the Church of the Nazarene in the mid-1950s in the belief that Nazarenes had grown worldly. The realization that the 1956 General Assembly would not ban television viewing by Nazarenes was one of the precipitating factors. The Bible Missionary Church's early membership was not drawn solely from Nazarene circles but also attracted people from other larger Holiness denominations. Glenn Griffith, a former Nazarene district superintendent, was an early leader but left the Bible Missionary Church because it allowed divorced Christians into membership, a stance he opposed.

The church operates Bible Missionary Institute at Rock Island, Illinois, and publishes the *Missionary Revivalist*. It rejects most 20th-century Bible translations and champions the use of the King James Version.

Brethren in Christ

The River Brethren emerged from successive waves of revivalism flowing through Pennsylvania's German-American communities in the late 1700s. Like Mennonites and German Baptist Brethren, they adhered to a strong believers' church ideology and embraced Christian pacifism. But they disagreed with Mennonites on the mode of baptism and with German Baptist Brethren on baptism's significance in the Christian life. Thus they chose an independent path. The Brethren in Christ name was adopted in the mid-19th century.

The Brethren in Christ Church cultivates ties to both Anabaptist and Wesleyan traditions. It participates in Mennonite World Fellowship and the compassionate ministries of Mennonite Central Committee, yet it also belongs to Christian Holiness Partnership. Messiah College in Grantham, Pennsylvania, is its primary educational institution.

Evangelical Friends

Evangelical Friends International is a fellowship of Quaker Yearly Meetings (state organizations) that embrace the Wesleyan view of entire sanctification. Evangelical Friends constitute one of the four basic divisions within the American Quaker community that are discussed in another chapter. The Ohio, Kansas, and Northwest Yearly Meetings are among the bodies composing the Evangelical Friends.

George Fox University in Oregon and Friends University in Kansas are among the Quaker schools related in varying degrees to the Holiness Movement.

Christian and Missionary Alliance

Several noted American Holiness revivalists preached in England in the mid-19th century. As a result, an annual convention was founded in Keswick, England, to perpetuate the message of a second and deeper work of God's grace subsequent to conversion.

But the Keswick view of holiness differs in ways from the Wesleyan-Holiness preaching that gave rise to it. The Keswick Convention emphasizes the baptism of the Holy Spirit as an experience of power for Christian living and service, but it rejects Wesleyan theology's insistence that entire sanctification represents a cleansing from original sin. Keswickians teach that the baptism of the Holy Spirit suppresses sin but does not cleanse it from the heart. This became a type of holiness for mild Calvinists. Revivalists associated with D. L. Moody brought Keswick theology from England to America in the late 19th century.

The Christian and Missionary Alliance is the sole denomination that exists to perpetuate Keswick teaching. It was founded by A. B. Simpson, a Presbyterian, in 1897. Simpson preached a fourfold gospel of Jesus as "Savior, Sanctifier, Healer, and Coming King." The formula represents a doctrinal core centered in conversion, sanctification, divine healing, and the premillennial second coming of Christ. The CMA has nearly 187,000 full members in North America. Its inclusive membership (children and associate members) is nearly 390,000. Its worldwide membership has been estimated at over 2 million.[8]

A Relevant Tradition for the Modern World

What role does the Wesleyan-Holiness tradition play in the modern world? Does it have resources for meeting human need, or is it just another circle of heart-happy pietists sitting over in the corner, holding hands, and singing "Heavenly Sunshine"?

Holiness people are indeed heart-happy pietists, but not irrelevant ones.

Late Harvard-trained historian (and Nazarene minister) Timothy L. Smith drew attention to the socially positive aspects of revivalistic perfectionism in his classic study of mid-19th-century religion, *Revivalism and Social Reform* (1955). He showed that Christians of perfectionist persuasion played important roles in the campaign against slavery. They also identified with the concerns of the poor and helped raise the status of women to equality with men. His pioneering historical study was coupled with the pleas for compassion in Carl F. H. Henry's *Uneasy Conscience of Modern Fundamentalism* (1947) and David O. Moberg's *Great Reversal* (1972). Together these three writings played a key role in the revival of Evangelical social responsibility after World War II. The rebirth of Nazarene Compassionate Ministries in the 1980s was one of the happy consequences as Nazarenes and other Wesleyans renewed their covenant with their own founding principles.

Other writers also draw freely from this tradition, including Howard Snyder, author of *The Problem of Wine Skins, The Radical Wesley, Community of the King, Liberating the Church,* and other titles. Snyder's works deal with contemporary issues in the Church and always address a wide audience. But he also writes from a perspective shaped by the spiritual and ethical resources of his own Free Methodist Church and the broader Wesleyan-Holiness tradition.

Similar commitments shape the writings of Donald W. Dayton (*Discovering an Evangelical Heritage,* 1976), a member of The Wesleyan Church, and Nazarene pastor Michael J. Christensen (*City Streets, City People,* 1988, and *The Samaritan's Imperative,* 1991). Ronald J. Sider, a Brethren in Christ theologian, is the founder of Evangelicals for Social Action and the author of *Rich Christians in an Age of Hunger* (1977). Sider is more self-consciously shaped by the Anabaptist side of his denomination, but John Wesley would have little trouble endorsing Sider's book on Christian responsibility in an era of great spiritual and human need.

A pietist tradition? Yes. And one, we trust, that is fit for citizenship in both heaven and earth.

PART 3

THE LITURGICAL CHURCHES

AT A GLANCE

THE EASTERN ORTHODOX CHURCHES

Historical Roots

All Christians trace their faith back to Jesus and the apostles. But the Eastern Orthodox believers do so directly. Some Orthodox congregations can trace their origins back to the very presence in their own city of the apostles themselves. Christianity was conceived in the East, was born in the East, and spent its childhood there before venturing westward.

Most Christians in the Middle East, Turkey, Greece, the Balkan countries, Ukraine, and Russia belong to the Orthodox tradition.

Core Beliefs

Orthodoxy is the church of the crucial councils of the early Christian centuries. The Orthodox believe in the Trinity, the person and divinity of Jesus Christ, and the full divinity of the Holy Spirit as described by the councils of Nicaea and Chalcedon. They believe the seven church councils are the unchangeable, infallible authority for the church, even outranking the Bible.

Orthodoxy teaches that Christ was the Second Adam, and the "All-Holy, immaculate, most blessed and glorified Lady, Mother of God, and Ever-Virgin Mary" was the Second Eve. The goal of redemption is sanctification, or Christian perfection.

Agreement and Differences

Nazarenes agree with Orthodox believers on the nature of the Trinity, the Holy Spirit, and Jesus Christ. We have built on their views of Christian perfection as interpreted by John Wesley. We agree with them about heaven and hell, and about personal responsibility and free will. We differ on the Bible. Nazarenes affirm it to be the highest authority. Orthodoxy sees the Bible as subordinate to tradition. We differ in the mode of worship and on the manner in which redeeming grace is received. In the Orthodox way an infant may receive baptism for remission of sin, chrismation for receiving the Holy Spirit, and then receive first Communion—all in the same service. They trust not in a personal experience or encounter with God for salvation, but upon the eternal power of the church to declare one redeemed.

Orthodoxy Today

More martyrs have died for their faith in the 20th century than in all preceding ones. Most Christians dying for their faith in this century have been Orthodox victims of Communism. There are about 160 million Orthodox believers today, 5 million in North America.

"God became man so that man could become god."

—Athanasius

CHAPTER 6

THE EASTERN ORTHODOX CHURCHES

WHAT DO YOU THINK OF when someone speaks of a "fast-growing church"? A megachurch in a megalopolis with a pastor and a program tuned into the consumerized "full-service church" frenetically giving the customer whatever he or she wants? How about an ancient church, as old as Christianity itself, with an ancient liturgy given in an ancient language?

Eastern Orthodoxy forms one of the fastest-growing religious bodies in North America. The church sign may read Greek Orthodox, Russian Orthodox, Serbian Orthodox, Orthodox Church in America, or something else. There are 160 million Orthodox believers in the world. When you add their "cousins" in the five related non-Chalcedon churches, the total is near 187 million Christians.[1]

America's growing Orthodox presence now approaches 5 million. Greek Orthodox believers account for half. Orthodox worship services are carried on in ethnic languages, yet Americans are being drawn to the various Orthodox denominations. Patrick Reardon says, "It is incredible but nonetheless true that a couple of million Americans now regularly worship in ancient Greek, Arabic, or church Slavonic, of which they do not understand one word in a hundred."[2]

What is their appeal? For one thing, in this scatterbrained world of "isms" galore, Eastern Orthodoxy provides the stability of a tradition nearly 2,000 years old. Orthodox churches are changeless if anything, basing their creeds on the earliest Christian councils. Their goal is "to preserve the Doctrine of the Lord uncorrupted, and firmly adhere to the Faith He delivered to us . . . neither adding any thing, nor taking any thing from it."[3] Talk about stability—"There are congregations today that trace their origins to the very presence, in their own cities, of Jesus' apostles."[4] Given the fact that Christianity started in the East and moved west, the Eastern Church is "the mother of us all." Returning to Christian roots is what many people want, and some find those roots in Orthodoxy.

Further, the Orthodox treasure "a deep sense of divine mystery in worship."[5] For contemporary children of the Enlightenment, overdosed on rationality, analysis, and technology, the holy mysteries have a lot of appeal.

Some are attracted to the hierarchical authority of the Orthodox Church. Tired of each person being a law unto himself or herself, they find security in the way the Orthodox recognize and obey church authorities. Neither theology nor church polity is put to popular vote.

Another attraction draws people to Orthodoxy: love for the arts. Icons, statuary, paintings, and architecture fill a void in hearts starved for aesthetics. How different from the Evangelical and Fundamentalist approaches that often wage war on the arts!

The worship service in Orthodox churches appeals to many in our fragmented world. They won't wonder whether there will be a chancel drama, a Christian rap group, a sports celebrity, or a Sandi Patty concert at church this Sunday. Every Sunday has its special place in the Christian year with its own liturgy. Another thing that appeals to this generation of Americans is the Orthodox teaching that the aim of the Christian life is to become so like God that you yourself become divine or deified. The longing after divinization of human nature, for holiness, so distorted by New Age silliness, finds Christian foundations in Orthodox teachings.

Orthodox and Nazarene Beliefs Compared

At some points Nazarenes will say "Yea and amen" to the doctrines of Orthodoxy. At other points we will differ with conviction and respect.

Tradition

Nazarenes treasure their traditions, but the Orthodox prize theirs far more. They believe that the holy tradition handed to them must be preserved inviolate. For them, tradition includes several things: the creeds of the seven infallible ecumenical councils, the teachings of the church fathers, the canon laws, the liturgy service books, the holy icons, and the books of the Bible (including the apocryphal books). "Orthodox Christians of today see themselves as heirs and guardians to a rich inheritance . . . and they believe it is their duty to transmit this inheritance unimpaired to the future."[6]

In Eastern Orthodoxy the Bible is just one part of an authoritative tradition. It stands on par with the creeds, the laws, the fathers, and the liturgy, but it does not stand above them. This is distinctly different from the Protestant doctrine of *sola scriptura,* or Scripture as the sole rule of faith. Nazarenes are thoroughly Protestant in their view of the Bible as the final Arbiter on matters of doctrine and practice. Thus, while we admire the loyalty to their tradition demonstrated by the Orthodox, we still choose to give the Bible preeminence. While they believe the councils and creeds to be infallible and unchangeable, we give such status only to the Bible.

The Doctrine of God

Nazarenes believe that "God is Triune in essential being, revealed as Father, Son, and Holy Spirit."[7] By that, we mean that there is one divine essence, three distinct Persons, with the divine essence totally indwelling each Person of the Trinity. We are not as concerned as Orthodoxy about the nuances of Trinitarian faith. For example, we can readily use the Nicene Creed (East) in one service and recite the Apostles' Creed (West) in the next and never know the difference.

The Orthodox believe that Western Christians emphasize the unity of God to the detriment of the distinct Persons. They also think that Catholics and Protestants denigrate the Holy Spirit by saying in the creed that He "proceeds" from both the Father and the Son and is therefore subordinate to the First and Second Persons of the Trinity.

Ted Campbell examined creedal statements in Orthodox literature and summarized the Orthodox view of the Trinity: "God is three 'Persons' in one 'substance.' . . . The three Persons differ in their 'modes of origin' (the Father is unbegotten, the Son is begotten, and the Spirit proceeds), and . . . the three Persons 'interpenetrate' each other in all acts of God."[8]

Nazarenes would agree with the Orthodox that wherever God is at work, it is the work of the Holy Trinity and not the work of an "errand boy" sort of deity. We would also agree with them that God is transcendent (different from us, and beyond our ability to comprehend Him) but also personal and incarnate.

Jesus Christ

Both Nazarenes and Orthodox agree on the basic definition of the nature of Christ. Orthodox Christians would like the Nazarene affirmation that Christ is "the Second Person of the Triune Godhead; that He was eternally one with the Father; that He became incarnate by the Holy Spirit and was born of the Virgin Mary, so that *two whole and perfect natures,* that is to say the Godhead and manhood, are thus united in one Person very God and very man, the God-man."[9]

The Church of the Nazarene also agrees with Eastern Orthodoxy on the mission of Jesus, the Son of God. He came to save us from our sins. Sin obscured the path to God, but "Jesus Christ, by uniting humankind and God in His own person, reopened for us the path to union with God."[10] Jesus showed us what likeness to God looked like and "set that likeness once again within our reach. Christ, the Second Adam . . . reversed the effects of the first Adam's disobedience."[11]

But the Orthodox also want to speak a few words to us about the way we worship Christ. Why do you in the West, they would inquire, grieve so much over Christ the Victim rather than celebrate Christ the Victor? In Orthodox worship, the glory of the conquering Christ is celebrated with joy—every Sunday. Thus, the Transfiguration and the Resurrection are the highest holy events on the calendar. In the West, Christmas (the Incarnation) and Good Friday (the Crucifixion) far exceed the attention given to the Transfiguration. Both traditions, however, make the Resurrection central to the faith.

There is more than aesthetics at stake here in the Orthodox mind. They believe that the Catholic and Protestant worshipers spend too much time trying to sympathize and agonize with the suffering Savior, that Western Christians see the Crucifixion too much in legal terms, with Jesus trying to satisfy an angry Father God and to "pay the penalty" for us. When the Orthodox meditate on the Crucifixion, they are more likely to concentrate on Christ in an act of love conquering sin, death, and hell in our behalf. Their hearts turn to praise rather than morbid agonizing before the Cross. Do they have something to teach us?

The Holy Spirit

"Christ's work of redemption cannot be considered apart from the Holy Spirit's work of sanctification," writes Orthodox Bishop Timothy Kallistos Ware.[12] He goes on to say, "From one point of view, the whole 'aim' of the Incarnation is the sending of the Spirit at Pentecost."[13] Russian Seraphim of Sarov declared, "The true aim of the Christian life is the acquisition of the Holy Spirit of God."[14] Surely Nazarene believers everywhere would resonate with such proclamations.

At the beginning of each day, the devout Orthodox Christian recites the morning prayer that includes these words:

O heavenly King, O Comforter, the Spirit of Truth, everywhere present and filling all things, the treasury of blessings and giver of life, come and abide in us. Cleanse us from all impurity, and of [by] Your goodness save our souls.[15]

Though Nazarenes and Orthodox differ on how to receive the

fullness of the Spirit, they are on the same page when it comes to articulating the doctrine of the Spirit. The Nazarene Articles of Faith include this affirmation: "We believe in the Holy Spirit . . . He is ever present and efficiently active in and with the Church of Christ, convincing the world of sin, regenerating those who repent and believe, sanctifying believers, and guiding into all truth as it is in Jesus."[16]

Mary, the Mother of Jesus

The Orthodox honor Mary as the most exalted human creature. She is, they believe, more glorious than the angels in heaven. Each time she is mentioned in the weekly liturgy, her full title is given: "Our All-Holy, immaculate, most blessed and glorified Lady, Mother of God, and Ever-Virgin Mary."[17]

"If Christ is the New Adam," writes Bishop Kallistos Ware, "Mary is the New Eve." He quotes Jerome: "Death by Eve, life by Mary."[18] While officially rejecting the Roman Catholic view of the Immaculate Conception, the Orthodox teaching and practice come very close to it.

Nazarenes, of course, must part company with our Orthodox friends here. In line with traditional Protestantism, believing in the priesthood of all believers, we honor the saints, the "faithful departed," but we do not pray to or through them in worship or venerate them with holy icons.

Humanity: Creation and Fall

Both Nazarene and Orthodox Christians believe that human beings are created in the likeness of God, as the Scripture teaches. Thus, we are "His kin," which means "that between us and Him there is a point of contact and similarity."[19] The Orthodox teach that the *likeness* of God in which Adam and Eve were created included *holiness, immortality, reason, and freedom* (the power and ability to do God's will). These terms define four attributes of God and describe what godliness is. The *likeness* of God, the Orthodox teach, was lost in the fall of Adam, and only the *image* remains. The *image* retained in all human beings consists of *reason and freedom.*[20]

Holiness and immortality were lost in the Fall. Therefore, the purpose of salvation and the quest of the Christian life are to regain what was lost: holiness and immortality.

Reason and freedom are retained, and with them comes the grace of God that makes it possible for persons to avoid sin and choose God. The Orthodox believe in free will and free grace. They dismiss the Calvinist doctrines of predestination, moral inability, and limited atonement. John Wesley's statements about free and prevenient grace and limited human freedom are very close to the Orthodox teachings.

The Orthodox and the Wesleyan-Arminian traditions share a strong belief in original sin. "In losing holiness they [our first parents] fell into sin; in losing immortality they became susceptible to disease, corruption and death."[21] These positions have been echoed by many theologians in our own Wesleyan-Holiness tradition.

Orthodoxy makes little or no attempt to describe the mystery of how original sin passes from generation to generation. No scientific study of genetics is suggested. They are content to teach that "cut off from God, Adam and his descendants passed under the domination of sin and of the devil. Each new human being is born into a world where sin prevails . . . a world in which it is easy to do evil and hard to do good."[22]

John Wesley taught, in harmony with Orthodoxy, that individuals are not personally guilty for Adam's sin. They bear the marks of that sin but do not carry the guilt. Each one of us is responsible for his or her own sins.

The Wesleyan-Holiness tradition holds another doctrine about original sin that is in common with Orthodoxy. Wesleyanism and Orthodoxy both teach that the results of the Fall extend to every part of the person, affecting all areas of life (the mind is darkened, the will enfeebled, and so on). That is to say that the likeness or image of God is impaired but not crushed or destroyed, as some teach. Bishop Ware writes, "Orthodox do not say as Calvin said, that human beings after the fall are utterly depraved and incapable of good desires. They cannot agree with Augustine . . . that human beings are under a 'harsh necessity' of committing sin . . . and . . . lack freedom."[23]

The Aim of Salvation

The aim of salvation for the Orthodox is "godlikeness," or to use their own language, *theosis*, meaning "deification" or "divinization." To the Catholic Christian and the Reformed believer, this sounds incredibly arrogant. To the New Age devotee, it sounds like a pleasing self-fulfillment dictum.

But Orthodox thinkers past and present have taken seriously the words of Scripture that say, for example, "Jesus answered, 'Is it not written in your law, "I said, you are gods"?'" (John 10:34, NRSV). He was quoting Ps. 82:6: "You are gods, children of the Most High, all of you" (NRSV). And what of Christ's high-priestly prayer?—"That they may all be one. As you, Father, are in me and I am in you, may they also be in us" (John 17:21, NRSV).

In addition to scriptural authority, the Eastern fathers (held to be equals or near equals with Scripture in the infallible tradition) taught that "God became man so that man could become god." These words of Athanasius were restated by several others, including Irenaeus.[24] Basil defined a Christian as one who had received the command to become a god. The Orthodox liturgy for Holy Thursday includes these words attributed to Christ: "In my kingdom . . . I shall be God with you as gods."[25]

Therefore, for the Orthodox, salvation and redemption mean to become so godlike that divinization or Christian perfection is not a misnomer. They do not believe that this happens all at once, but that it takes a lifetime of devotion to attain as the believer works in cooperation with the Holy Spirit.

There is a unique connection between the Orthodox teaching of theosis and the Wesleyan doctrine of entire sanctification. John Wesley did not import this doctrine whole, but he found in the teachings of the Eastern fathers sure foundations for his teaching of Christian perfection, holiness, or entire sanctification.[26] Wesley was so impressed by the teachings of perfect love and sanctification he studied in the Eastern fathers that he reprinted several of their works and made them required reading for his preachers and recommended reading for laypersons who were serious about the pursuit of holiness.

Careful scholars note that Wesley stopped well short of endorsing theosis, the deification of the believer. Without the foundations of the Orthodox fathers, however, Wesley would have had to search for a new vocabulary for his pastoral theology. What Wesley did find in them that he transplanted into Methodism was a radical optimism of grace that declares that there is almost no ceiling on the good things that can happen in, to, and through the sanctified believer.

Wesley saw in the Eastern fathers a high degree of Christian perfection or holiness that he believed could be lived by ordinary Christians in the workaday world. In both East and West it was taught that those in holy orders who have endless time for devotion are the ones who can live lives holy and acceptable to God. Though stopping short of the doctrine of deification, Wesley believed and preached that ordinary people can be entirely sanctified, living holy lives.

Whether it is a Wesleyan speaking of entire sanctification or an Orthodox Christian speaking of deification, one question about reaching this goal needs to be asked: How do good works, acts of piety and acts of mercy, relate to the obtaining or attaining of the end of salvation?

When Wesleyans speak of the restoration of the image of God (entire sanctification), they are thoroughly Protestant. Both justifying and sanctifying grace come *sola gratia*, that is, by grace alone. Wesley taught that works of piety and mercy are necessary in a secondary way, but certainly not meritorious. No number of deeds of piety or service can sanctify a believer. Only God does that as a gift of grace through faith.

Orthodoxy, while maintaining a high view of grace, makes good works essential to achieving deification or holiness. Though the ability to achieve good works is a gift of grace itself, the performance of them is somewhat meritorious in *attaining* holiness. Protestants are troubled by the role that the Orthodox give to *attaining* or *achieving* deification, divinization, or Christian perfection. Wesleyans speak of *obtaining* holiness or sanctification as a gift of grace through faith, but they stop short of teaching that holiness can be *attained*.

Receiving Salvation

We have seen that strong similarities exist between the Orthodox and Wesleyan traditions when it comes to the doctrines and aims of salvation. They are not nearly so compatible when it comes to how to receive saving and sanctifying grace.

To begin with, the Wesleyans (and believers of all other churches in the Augustinian tradition) have a lot to say about justification by faith alone. The Orthodox are not nearly so concerned about such forensic matters. They speak often of forgiveness of sins, but sparingly of justification.

The entry into the Christian life is also quite different in the two traditions. Evangelical Wesleyans (such as the Church of the Nazarene and the Holiness Movement) insist that entry into the true Christian life comes through a conversion experience, a personal encounter with the living Christ involving confession, repentance, and saving faith. For the Orthodox (as well as for Roman Catholics and classical Protestants), the entry into the Christian life occurs at baptism—whether as an adult or infant.

Throughout the whole order of salvation, the Wesleyans and the Orthodox represent widely differing views. The Orthodox depend on the "infallible" tradition, apostolic authority, and the sacred liturgy of the church. They strongly believe that salvation has nothing to do with how they feel or what they may individually experience. In their view, they know they are saved because of the holy, infallible word of the true Church. Since God has given the church the authority to dispense saving and sanctifying grace, why not do it as soon as the infant is able to appear? Thus, the infant is baptized for remission of sin, receives chrismation (a ceremony in which it is believed the infant receives sanctifying grace and the gift of the Spirit), and then receives his or her first Communion—all in the same service.

Most Wesleyans would feel that to do this is to put far too much emphasis on the authority of the church to declare who is and who isn't in a state of grace.

Though some Wesleyans have always permitted infant baptism, it has never been meant to take the place of a personal conversion experience when the individual reaches the age of accountability. Further, the gift of the sanctifying Spirit cannot be bestowed by any church ceremony, Wesleyans believe. The Wesleyan tradition is, for better or worse, a system that values saving and sanctifying encounters with the living God, that is, certain types of religious experiences, far more than it values creedal or ecclesiastical authority.

Heaven and Hell

Both Wesleyan and Orthodox Christians believe in eternal rewards and punishments—heaven and hell. The Orthodox counter objections that the existence of hell would slur the reputation of a loving God by pointing out that since we have free will, it is possible to reject God. As stated in Ware's book, "Hell is nothing else than the rejection of God. . . . Hell is not so much a place where God imprisons humans, as a place where humans, by misusing their free will, choose to imprison themselves."[27]

Worship and the Sacraments

We have already discussed baptism, believed by the Orthodox to bring forgiveness of sin. Baptism is by immersion in Orthodoxy. The person is immersed three times, once for each Person of the Trinity. Seldom is baptism by another Christian church recognized as valid by Orthodoxy. And baptism "by sprinkling or smearing is quite simply not real Baptism at all."[28] Wesleyans usually permit the baptismal candidate to select the method of baptism preferred. Further, if a person has been baptized by another Christian church, Wesleyans recognize it as valid and do not rebaptize.

Holy Communion, or the Eucharist, is a rich tradition in the Orthodox Church. Only those who are Orthodox can receive it, and only those Orthodox who have prepared by fasting are expected to participate. The bread is leavened, not unleavened. The bread and wine are understood to be the true body and blood of Christ. The Communion elements become, for the Orthodox worshiper, a sacrifice. And since Christ is considered present in the elements, the sacrifice offered is once again Christ himself. And this sacrifice is offered to the Holy Trinity in behalf of the living and the dead.

In the Wesleyan tradition, Holy Communion is offered to all believers, regardless of church membership. The bread and the wine are understood to be symbols of the body and blood of our Lord.

Wesleyans celebrate two sacraments: baptism and Holy Communion. The Orthodox add five more: chrismation, confession, holy orders, marriage, and the anointing of the sick.

Worship among the Wesleyans usually follows the free church style, with a wide variety of practices ranging from low church Anglican liturgical style to largely unplanned evangelical or charismatic modes. Orthodox worship is, of course, highly liturgical. Every day of the Christian year has specific significance, whether it is St. James Day on October 23 or Mary the Mother of God Day on August 15 or Circumcision of Christ Day on January 1. The service books prescribing Orthodox liturgies throughout the year take up 20 volumes.

There are 12 great festivals (feasts) during the year. Seven of them are feasts celebrating Jesus; five honor Mary. A number of minor festivals are also celebrated, such as the one in honor of St. Nicolas the Wonderworker on December 6 and the nativity of St. John the Baptist on June 24.

Since the Orthodox also believe that "fasting and self-control are the first virtue, the mother, root, source and foundation of all good," their calendar is punctuated with five great fasts.[29]

Worship is conducted without benefit of pews. The congregation stands during the entire service. In America, the typical service runs for one to two hours. But in earlier times, people usually stood through a seven- or eight-hour service. No musical instruments are used in Orthodox services, but the service is sung or chanted.

The Church

The Orthodox Church believes that it is the one true Church. Some say this with Christian humility. They are quick to say that this does not make them better than other people. That they belong to the one true Church is but a gift of grace. They may cite the words of Metropolitan Eulogy: "Have not the saints passed beyond the walls that separate us, walls which . . . do not mount up as high as heaven."[30] They are also likely very active in national and international ecumenical meetings. On the other hand, some Orthodox simply tell you that there is no salvation outside their "one true Church."

While some Wesleyan-Holiness groups may have acted as if *they* were the one true Church, it has never been their creed. It is hard to find a tradition that has been more ecumenical than the Wesleyan. From John Wesley's sermons "Against Bigotry" and "The Catholic Spirit" on to the present day, Wesleyans have extended the right hand of fellowship to almost all who believe in the Bible and in Christ as Savior.

AT A GLANCE

THE ROMAN CATHOLIC CHURCH

Historical Roots

The Christians who spread through the Roman Empire called themselves the "catholic" (universal) church. As the bishop of Rome rose in significance, the "catholic" church in the western Mediterranean took on a Roman identity. With the official split between Eastern and Western Christians, the Roman Catholic Church became the church of western Europe. Eventually it also spread to Africa, Asia, and the Americas. Claiming that Peter was the first pope, the Roman Catholic Church has 1 billion members and is the largest Christian body in the world.

Core Beliefs

Roman Catholics believe in the triune God and in Jesus Christ, the Son of God, born of a virgin, and Savior of the world. They believe in the person and work of the Holy Spirit. They venerate Mary as "the Mother of God" and the only human being (except Jesus) to be born without original sin. Catholics believe theirs is the one true Church, but God will be merciful to Protestants. They honor the Bible as inspired, but it does not outrank Catholic authorities. Catholics oppose premarital sex, homosexual activity, birth control, and abortion.

Agreement and Differences

Nazarenes are in harmony with Roman Catholicism on the doctrines of the Trinity, Christ, the Holy Spirit, sin, and redemption. Differences arise over the place of the Bible. We do not venerate Mary or proscribe birth control, but we do oppose abortion, homosexual activity, and adultery. As Protestants, we affirm salvation by grace alone through faith. Catholics see grace as the primary means of salvation, but they believe that one must partially pay for salvation through various disciplines, service, and suffering. Nazarenes also disagree with the Catholic dogma of confession to a priest.

Roman Catholics Today

One person out of every six in our world is a Roman Catholic. Twenty-three percent of the United States population identified themselves as Catholics in 1993.

"Our past embraces the good, the bad, and the ordinary, and we who are Catholic accept it all as ours. We trace ourselves back to the Church of the Apostles. . . . There have been Judases in the Church in every age, but there have been far more saints. . . . Our lives, our histories, are . . . the Catholic Church, the Body of Christ."

—Father Oscar Lukefahr
The Privilege of Being Catholic

CHAPTER 7

THE ROMAN CATHOLIC CHURCH

THOUGH OUTCAST AND OUTLAWED, the early Christians conquered the Roman Empire. The Holy Spirit descended on the 120 believers on the Day of Pentecost and set that little community of faith ablaze with evangelical fire. When the hammer of persecution struck the Jerusalem church like an anvil, the sparks of divine fire showered the Mediterranean world as those heroes of faith went everywhere preaching the gospel. That church, like Jesus, belongs to all of us who take the name Christian.

That church called itself the "catholic" or "universal" Church of Jesus Christ at least as early as A.D. 110. Ignatius of Antioch in his *Epistle to the Smyrnaeans* wrote, "Wherever Jesus Christ is present, we have the catholic Church."[1] Polycarp, the martyred bishop of Smyrna, wrote in A.D. 156 of "the holy catholic church."[2] And Cyprian of Carthage about A.D. 250 wrote a treatise titled *The Unity of the Catholic Church.*[3]

The Roman Catholics

The Roman Catholic Church is the community of faith that developed in western Europe after the Edict of Milan in 312. At that time Emperor Constantine saw a vision of the Cross and was told, "By this sign conquer." Though he was not baptized until the day of his death, his edict made Christianity a legal religion in the empire.

Christian growth accelerated. Centers of Christian influence developed in Alexandria, Antioch, Byzantium, Carthage, Ephesus, and Rome. Bishops in the West came to recognize the bishop of Rome as "first among equals." While heresies flourished in Asia and North Africa, Rome built a reputation as the champion of orthodox doctrines.

The Christian Church hammered out its orthodoxy at seven ecumenical councils held between 325 and 787. The early ones at Nicaea, Constantinople, Ephesus, and Chalcedon clarified the doctrines of the Trinity and the divine/human nature of Christ—dogmas that still form basic Christian beliefs. After these councils, however, the church in the East (Eastern Orthodoxy) and the church in the West (Roman Catholicism) drifted increasingly apart administratively and doctrinally.

The Council of Trent

Eastern Orthodoxy and Roman Catholicism had long separated by the time the Council of Trent opened in 1545. It lasted 18 years and produced more legislation than all former general councils recognized by the Roman Church.

Trent blamed the Protestant Reformation on the "ambition, avarice, and cupidity" of high-ranking clergy and condemned the works of Luther, Zwingli, and Calvin.[4] Roman Catholic views that had emerged in the Middle Ages were reinforced against such Protestant principles as *sola scriptura*. Catholics assumed that Scripture alone was not enough, since the church existed before the Bible, created the Bible, and had jurisdiction over its interpretation.

Trent also struck down *sola fide*. Faith alone was not enough to bring salvation. Even popes "have to earn their way to salvation like any other Catholic."[5] *Sola gratia* was also denounced. Salvation was indeed by grace but could not be achieved without penitential works and the sacraments administered in the one true Catholic Church.

The Council of Trent preserved the pope as monarch, the seven sacraments, the Latin sacrificial mass, indulgences, icons, veneration of saints, confession to priests, and the primacy of church tradition over Scripture. "The council's work was essentially medieval; only the anger was new."[6] That anger was expressed in inquisitions, civil wars, and persecutions as both sides declared themselves the true Church.

Trent made some productive administrative decisions. Bishops were to live holy lives. Seminaries were to be established. The council abolished the position of "indulgence seller." The Roman Catholic Church began to grow remarkably in the wake of Trent and other revival efforts.

The Modern Roman Catholic Councils

Two general councils of the Roman Catholic Church have transpired since the Council of Trent. Vatican I was held in 1869-70 in Rome under Pope Pius IX's direction. Vatican I reinforced the idea of the pope as a prince of the church. It made the doctrine of papal infallibility a specific dogma. Eighty-four bishops opposed the original legislation, and 55 bishops formally absented themselves on the final vote.[7] The vote carried, however, and Catholics ever since are required to believe that when the pope makes official announcements (speaks ex cathedra) about the church's faith and practice, it is the very voice of Peter and Christ, and that is infallible and not subject to challenge or change.

Vatican II, held in the 1960s, was much different. It was held *for* something, not *against* something. Pope John XXIII stated that its purpose was to bring the church up-to-date and make it relevant to everyday life. Most of the adjustments made were, in fact, steps toward Protestant principles.

1. The council moved toward democratizing aspects of the church, at least locally, by announcing that the laity had a priestly service to fulfill. After Vatican II, laity took over many local church functions previously reserved to the priests. This stops short of the full Protestant doctrine of the priesthood of all believers, but it is a step in that direction.

2. The liturgy was simplified. The mass was to be given in the language of the people—not in Latin.

3. While affirming the Roman Catholic Church as the true Church, Vatican II voiced official "respect" for Protestants. They were termed "separated brethren," not heretics. This was a radical change from Trent. Protestant churches could be a way to salvation, a preparation for the Kingdom. Even other religions could be a way to God. Vatican II regarded, as Catholic theologian Yves Congar put it, "religions as an ordinary way of salvation and Christianity as an extraordinary way."[8]

4. Scripture was given more prominence as the rule for faith and practice. It did not rise above tradition, councils, and ex cathedra pronouncements by the pope, but it was elevated to first among equals. Lay Bible study was strongly encouraged for the first time. Since then, many Catholics have participated in an explosion of small-group Bible studies.

5. The infallibility of the pope was muted by an equal emphasis on the importance and authority of the council of bishops.

The Roman Catholic Church remains an absolute monarchy. The

pope is the only elected official. Yet Vatican II let in a greater measure of democratic principles.[9]

These changes were so dramatic that many Catholics were not prepared for them. Conservatives thought the changes added up to compromise with the Protestants' heretic and secular opinion. Many thought that the moves, while elevating the laity, diminished the priesthood. Some 8,000 American priests left the ministry between 1966 and 1972, and enrollments in Catholic seminaries in America decreased by 31 percent during those years.[10] Roman Catholicism has had an identity crisis since Vatican II.

Catholics and Protestants have worked together in interesting ways since Vatican II. Does this foreshadow a time when Christianity will once again be united?

A Survey of Roman Catholic Beliefs

1. Do Catholics believe in the triune God?

Yes. The orthodox beliefs about the Holy Trinity, forged in the early ecumenical councils, are affirmed by Roman Catholics and most Protestant churches, including the Church of the Nazarene.

2. Do Catholics believe that Jesus was fully human and yet fully God? That is, do they believe in the Incarnation?

Yes. They clearly teach orthodox doctrines about the Incarnation and the nature of Jesus Christ.

3. Do Catholics believe that the Holy Spirit is fully God?

Yes. Roman Catholics repeatedly affirm the divinity of the Third Person of the Trinity, the Holy Spirit. Nazarenes have no stronger ally on this issue.

4. Do Catholics believe in the virgin birth and resurrection of Jesus?

Yes. They refer to the Gospel of Luke and the Gospel of Matthew in support of the Incarnation, as do we. Catholics also teach the real, bodily resurrection of Jesus Christ.

5. Do Catholics view Mary the mother of Jesus the same way that Nazarenes do?

No. They call her *theotokos*, the "Mother of God," rather than the mother of Christ. This label was intended to protect the divinity of Jesus against certain early heresies. Catholics teach the Immaculate Conception. On December 8, 1854, Pope Pius IX defined the doctrine that Mary was the only human born without original sin. Catholic theology taught that original sin is passed genetically from generation to generation. Thus the Immaculate Conception of Mary was viewed as necessary to make the birth of the divine Son of God possible. Mary, they say, was without sin and "full of grace" from her conception. Thus she was free from the bent to sinning. "Therefore, Mary in holiness surpassed the beautitude of Adam and Eve and the angels who were capable of sin, while Mary was not."[11] Catholic catechist Oscar Lukefahr says that "the Immaculate Conception is an example of Catholic doctrine that is not clearly taught in Scripture but which, congruent with Scripture, was believed universally by Catholics for centuries before it was formally defined as doctrine by the pope."[12]

6. Do Catholics pray to Mary?

Yes, but not in the same way that they pray to God. They claim to *worship* God but only *venerate* Mary. They believe that given Mary's special status as the mother of God, she can help them by interceding with her Son in their behalf. Thus, they often pray for her to pray for them. She has a special place above all saints. She is viewed as the "new Eve"—just as Jesus is seen as the "new Adam"—without sin and the spiritual mother of us all. "Vatican II taught explicitly . . . that Mary is one of us, a member of the Church, and one of those redeemed by Christ."[13] This statement seems to humanize rather than further deify Mary.

7. What else do Catholics teach about Mary that is different from what most Protestants teach?

Catholics teach that Mary remained a virgin throughout her life. They regard the brothers of Jesus mentioned in the Bible as spiritual brothers, or children of Joseph by a former marriage. They also believe in the Assumption of Mary. The only ex cathedra pronouncement of a pope in the last 100 years included the teaching that at the end of Mary's life Christ gave her victory over death, and since she had never sinned, she was "assumed" or "translated" directly to heaven into complete union with her Son.[14]

8. Do Catholics pray to other saints?

They prefer the term *veneration* over *prayer* or *worship*, but prayer to deceased persons is a common practice among Catholics. "We pray to God—Father, Son, and Holy Spirit—as the source of all blessings," writes Oscar Lukefahr. "We pray to the saints in the sense that we ask them to pray with us and for us, to be near us in love and friendship and to lead us closer to Jesus."[15] To the Catholic mind, the line between the living and the dead is very faint. Persons alive or dead are considered church members whom we can ask to pray for us, much as you might ask your pastor to remember you in prayer. Among Protestants, the doctrine of the "priesthood of all believers" replaces this kind of mediation practice.

9. What do Catholics teach about the sacrament of the Lord's Supper?

The Lord's Supper (Holy Communion, Eucharist) is an area where Catholics and Protestants have always disagreed. Both practice this holy sacrament, but they disagree about what goes on during the service. Catholics insist that the bread and wine actually become the real body and blood of Jesus. Most Protestants regard the bread and wine (or juice) as *symbols* of Jesus' broken body and shed blood.

Both traditions encourage spiritual examination before receiving the sacrament. Fasting and confession to the priest of any mortal sin must precede Communion for Catholic believers. The sacrament also nourishes spiritual life, draws us closer to God and to each other, and foreshadows the return of our Lord. For Catholics, it is also a sacrifice that occurs during the mass. Drawing on the idea of the Passover lamb, whose blood saved the Israelites, Catholics see the Eucharist as a sacrifice for their own sins. The real Christ is present in the bread and wine, they believe, and the body and blood of Jesus are offered again to God as a holy sacrifice in payment for their sins.

In Catholic worship, the Eucharist is the central focus of the service. In Evangelical churches, the focus of the typical service is the sermon. Catholics believe that the real Christ is present in the sacrament offered again as a sacrifice for sin. Many Protestants and Evangelicals agree with Lutheran Dietrich Bonhoeffer that if the preacher faithfully preaches the saving words of Christ, the historical Christ is present, walking among the congregation, offering redemption. The end of both kinds of worship is to bring the worshiper to Christ in saving, reconciling relationship. The Catholic service does this through the *sacramental sacrifice*, the Evangelical through the sacrament of the *preached Word* and the invitation.

10. What does the Catholic Church teach about baptism?

Catholics teach that baptism brings four blessings: the forgiveness of sin (personal and original), regeneration (new life in Christ), union with God, and membership in the church. The rather elaborate ceremony includes baptism by immersion or pouring.

Though Catholics believe baptism is the occasion of forgiveness of sin, they do not say that baptism saves them. Baptism is necessary to salvation, but alone it does not save. Catholics are careful not to say they are "saved." That is Calvinistic Protestantism, they believe. Some Protestants say that once they have accepted Jesus as Lord and Savior, they are eternally saved. Catholics do not believe that salvation is a one-time-only affair. Instead of salvation as a singular experience, they see it as a journey. It is a journey begun in baptism, the first of three initiation sacraments. Baptism is followed by first Communion and then by confirmation. Oscar Lukefahr compares the journey of salvation to traveling by ship through the waters of this life to the safe haven of eternity. "The ship has been built. Christ has done everything necessary by his life, death, and resurrection to bring us to heaven. . . . But we must book passage on the ship and become an active part of the crew. We must 'work out' our salvation."[16] Lukefahr goes on to say, "The Bible shows that it is possible to 'jump ship' and choose the wrong destination."[17] Thus, Catholics will not say they are saved until they make it safely to heaven.

The Nazarene doctrine of baptism is not as complicated or as central to our Christian faith. We regard baptism as an outward sign of an inward grace. That grace is saving or justifying grace that comes in an encounter with Christ in which we confess and repent of our sins and put our trust in Jesus as Savior and Lord. After such a conversion experience, one may be baptized, thus testifying to all that he or she is a believer and wants to be known always as a disciple of Christ. Thus, baptism is not necessary, we believe, to salvation. What counts is a saving personal relationship with Jesus Christ. However, baptism is important as a blessing not to be missed. Our *Manual* states, "While we do not hold that baptism imparts the regenerating grace of God, we do believe that Christ gave this holy sacrament as a sign and seal of the new covenant."[18]

A fairly new program among Catholics is called the Rite of Christian Initiation of Adults. In this ministry the Catholics are returning to the ancient plan of preparing adult converts for baptism. It has four steps and may take several years. Step one is called the *Period of Inquiry,* in which the prospect learns the basic things about the faith. Step two is the *Catechumenate,* a period of more intensive instruction. Step three is *Enlightenment and Purification.* During Lent the candidate is led in study and prayer that climaxes at Easter with baptism, confirmation, and the holy Eucharist.[19] Often led by laymen as part of the new (1992) catechism, this program has been quite productive.

11. What is confirmation?

Confirmation is the third initiation rite that starts one on the path to heaven. Baptism brings forgiveness and regeneration, Catholics believe. Holy Communion is, among other things, a sacrament of sanctifying grace. Confirmation is also a sacrament of sanctification. More precisely, it is viewed as giving the gift of the Holy Spirit to the believer. "Confirmation is our Pentecost," one Catholic priest declares.[20] It brings the fruit of the Spirit and gives power for service. Nazarenes also believe in regeneration (saving grace) and sanctifying grace, but we regard these as personal experiences that a mere ceremony cannot usually deliver.

For Catholics, entry into the Christian life is something that happens over time. One catechist writes, "Conversion to Jesus Christ . . . is a fairly arduous event that takes time and the nurture of candidates by faith-filled members of the community."[21] Does it seem to you that Nazarenes can teach their Catholic brethren something about personal relationships with God, while *they* could teach *us* something about thoroughly preparing prospects for discipleship?

12. Do Catholics practice sacraments besides baptism and Holy Communion?

The Roman Catholic catechism lists seven sacraments categorized in this manner: three sacraments of initiation: baptism, Eucharist, and confirmation; two of healing: penance (or reconciliation) and the healing of the sick; and two of service and mission: holy orders and marriage. Most Protestant groups, including the Church of the Nazarene, recognize only baptism and Holy Communion as sacraments.

13. Do Catholics teach that salvation is by grace alone?

No. They do teach that grace is the primary source of salvation. Without God's gracious love and Christ's atonement, no one would have any hope of salvation. But given that, they teach that one earns, or partially pays for, salvation by his or her own works, piety, suffering, and service. By contrast, Protestant Calvinists and some Lutherans have declared that salvation is a matter of predestination. This underscores the belief that salvation depends on God and God alone, and nothing you do can make yourself worthy of salvation. Thus, classic Protestants speak of *obtaining* or *receiving* salvation. They never speak of *attaining* it or *achieving* it, as Catholics often do.

John Wesley, our spiritual ancestor, tried to find a middle road between the classic Protestant view of grace and Catholic view of works. He said that good works (acts of piety and acts of mercy) were necessary in a secondary sort of way, but that they never were to be regarded as earning or meriting salvation or even a little part of it. Good works were simply what any Christian should and would do. Wesley declared that he did not regard a person as having one grain of faith if he (or she) was not willing "to spend and be spent" for others.

14. What is the Catholic doctrine of penance?

Penance is a step in the Catholic practice of confession or reconciliation. First is *contrition*, or sorrow for one's sins. Second comes *confession* to a priest. Third, the priest weighs the offense and assigns a proper *satisfaction* or *penance*. This is an effort to make up for the damage one's sins have caused. The closest thing to this in Evangelical teaching is the practice of restitution: the convert is expected to pay back money that was stolen, apologize for falsehoods whispered, and so on.

In early centuries, Catholic penances were often severe. If after baptism a person committed adultery or engaged in homosexual acts, he or she was excommunicated for 15 years and commanded to totally abstain from sexual activity for the rest of his or her life. Homicide, sorcery, and incest were forgiven only after 20 years of repentant excommunication. Denying Christ under persecution was the gravest sin. The penance was segregation to the "weepers" part of the church for the rest of their lives, where they would mourn their sins in a loud voice every Sunday as the devout gathered for worship. They were not allowed to take Communion again—until the hour of their death.[22]

Things are much more lenient today, but the Catholic Church has a long history of accountability and penance. Contrition and confession are not enough; satisfaction must be made to God and one's fellow. After contrition, confession, and the assignment of penance, the priest grants *absolution*, or forgiveness of sins.

The Catholic view of purgatory is connected with penance. If one dies before performing all due penances, purgatorial fires will provide the suffering required and otherwise purify the soul, making the person ready for heaven eventually.

15. Why do most Protestants disagree with the idea of confessing sins to a priest?

Experience and wisdom indicate that there are times when confession to a Christian pastor or friend needs to be added to our confession to God. The Protestant principle of the priesthood of all believers includes the conviction that confession to God is what brings forgiveness and reconciliation. It is not up to a priest to tell us whether or not we are forgiven. The Bible promise is enough: "If we confess our sins, he is faithful and just to forgive us our sins" (1 John 1:9, KJV).

Part of the Protestant revolt against the Catholic confessional was that it gave priests too much control over one's life. When a mere human can give or withhold forgiveness and assign any punishment or penance that he pleases, dreadful abuses are all but guaranteed. Very

few if any Bible passages can be recruited to support the idea of confess-
ing to a priest, but Roman Catholic tradition upholds it.

The confessional can be abused in other ways. At the Synod of
Toledo in 589, this complaint was recorded: "We have heard that in
some churches in Spain the faithful . . . ask a priest to grant them pardon
as many times as it pleases them to sin."[23]

16. Do Catholics believe that the Bible is inspired?

Yes, but it carries less authority for them than it does for most
Protestants. We believe that the Bible is the final Authority on matters of
faith and salvation. Catholics hold that the church created the Bible for
its own use and therefore has power to interpret the Bible officially.
Though they view the Bible as the Word of God, they hold that church
tradition, infallible papal decrees, and theological councils have authority equal to that of the Scriptures.

17. Do Catholics believe that theirs is the one true Church?

Yes. Though they are reaching out to Protestants, Jews, and adherents of certain other religions, Vatican II says, "They could not be saved
who, knowing that the Catholic Church was founded as necessary by
God through Christ, would refuse to enter it, or to remain in it. . . . It is
through Christ's Church alone, which is the all-embracing means of salvation, that all fullness of the means of salvation can be obtained."[24] This
does not mean that Catholics believe that other Christians are going to be
lost eternally. Vatican II also said, "One cannot charge with the sin of separation those who at present are born into these communities [Protestant
churches] and in them were brought up in the faith of Christ, and the
Catholic Church accepts them with respect and affection as brothers."[25]

**18. Does the Catholic Church teach a biblical standard of sexual
morality?**

Yes. The Roman Catholic Church vigorously teaches against premarital sex, adultery, and homosexual activity. Catholics oppose abortion. The Catholic Church does not bless divorce. It warns members that
sex within marriage must be restrained and not lustful. On these matters the Church of the Nazarene and the Roman Catholic Church have
quite similar ideals.

The Catholic Church officially regards masturbation as a mortal
sin and prohibits artificial birth control. Nazarenes leave these two matters to individual conscience and pastoral guidance.

Recent polls show that most American Catholics do not share
their church's position on divorce, premarital sex, and birth control.[26]

The world's 1 billion Catholics total one-sixth of the human population. The Roman Catholic Church is by far the largest Christian body in the world. About 23 percent of Americans identified themselves as Catholics in 1993. United States Catholics number over 60 million and worship in about 20,000 churches.[27]

PART 4

CLASSICAL PROTESTANT CHURCHES

At a Glance

The First Protestants: Lutherans Rearrange the Christian World

Principal Leader

Martin Luther, Augustinian monk turned Reformer, was the uncontested leader of the Lutheran Reformation. He presided over the Reformation in Germany and influenced it in other countries. Luther and his disciples dramatically changed Christianity.

Core Beliefs

Justification by grace through faith in Christ.
The Bible as the Church's final Authority.
The priesthood of all believers—not just the ordained few.
The necessity of merging doctrine and spiritual experience.
The literal presence of Christ in the Communion elements.

Agreement and Differences

Nazarenes eagerly embrace the Protestant principles taught by Luther: justification by faith, salvation by grace not works, the authority of Scripture, and the priesthood of all believers.

We differ, however, on the nature of the Church, the Lord's Supper, baptism, worship styles, and the doctrine of sanctification.

Today's Lutheran Christians

Today there are 68 million Lutherans in 100 denominations worldwide. The largest American Lutheran body is the Evangelical Lutheran Church, with 5.2 million members.

Each man must do his own believing, just as each must do his own dying.

CHAPTER 8

THE FIRST PROTESTANTS: LUTHERANS REARRANGE THE CHRISTIAN WORLD

PROTESTANTISM EMERGED in the early 16th century as a new force in Christianity. It assumed four basic forms by 1600: Lutheranism, the Reformed (or Calvinist) tradition, Anabaptism, and Anglicanism. Each had its own genius, purpose, and spirit. And each contributed to the streams that have blended to create the Church of the Nazarene.

On the Road to Reformation

Lutheranism, like a wedge, cracked open Catholic Europe. It did not emerge in a vacuum. Sixteenth-century Europe was in ferment. Lutheranism was preceded by a renewed emphasis on preaching fostered in monastic orders founded by Dominic and Francis of Assisi. The Reformation, a product of this renewal, created Protestant churches that sustained and perpetuated the preaching revival.

Renaissance humanism also prepared the way for the Reformation. Catholic humanists preferred their theology with both feet on the ground. Some disdained abstract theology and studied Greek, Roman, and biblical literature instead of philosophy. Their research in ancient texts led to new methods of translation and study. This work on the Greek and Hebrew texts enabled Martin Luther and other Reformers to translate the Bible into the common languages of their day.[1]

Luther and the Reformation in Germany

Martin Luther was born in Saxony, a German state in the Holy Roman Empire. After taking a degree at the University of Erfurt, he became an Augustinian monk and priest. The Augustinians sent him to Wittenberg's new university for further study. There he completed an advanced degree and became professor of biblical theology.

But Luther was plagued by a terror of God. When he read Paul's words on the "justice of God," Luther felt judged and found guilty by the Great Judge. His anxiety did not lessen until he realized that the "justice of God" was not a doctrine of terror but one of liberation. God's justice is a judgment that frees, not condemns, the sinner. Luther came to understand that God's justice is one with God's acceptance of the sinner through grace.

Luther's new "theology of the Cross" emphasized humanity's radical sinfulness, the heart "turned in on itself" that makes one unable to be saved apart from God's grace. But Luther also emphasized God's radical decision to forgive sins. Christians are just because they are justified by God's grace through faith. This doctrine is called justification by faith. But grace—God's initiative—is its main point. Faith, for Luther, is the way God chooses to bestow saving grace. Faith is understood primarily as "trust" rather than "belief." Even devils believe in God—but of course, they don't place their *trust* in God!

The distinction between "law" and "gospel," derived from Paul, was important in Luther's theology. The doctrine of justification by grace cut through the legalism. Lutherans ever since have emphasized the distinction between law and gospel.

Ministry and Worship

Luther's theological breakthrough had implications for the Church and ministry. Roman Catholics drew a hard and fast line between clergy and laity. In Catholicism, marriage and ordination to the ministry are both sacraments, so men must choose one or the other (never both) as their service to God. But Luther argued that every Christian is a minister called by God through baptism to participate in the Church's ministry to the world. This idea was called the "priesthood of believers." Ordained clergy—set aside to preach, to administer the sacraments, and to lead the flock of Christ—represent the community of Christ and symbolize the whole Church's calling. The priesthood of believers makes us responsible ministers to one another and to the world. This doctrine also implied that laity should have some role in governing the church.

Luther believed that worship should be conducted in the people's own languages, so he edited Catholicism's Latin mass and translated it into German. He translated the Bible for the same reason. As Germans worshiped and read the Scriptures in their native tongue, a sense of nationhood slowly developed. A similar dynamic worked in other countries as Protestantism, for good or ill, reinforced the emerging European nationalism. It hastened the disintegration of the Holy Roman Empire, which had existed since Charlemagne in the ninth century.

Luther initiated many other changes that shape our lives as Protestants. Early Christians had accepted writings into the Old Testament that Jewish rabbis had not accepted into their canon. Luther excluded these writings, which Protestants call the Apocrypha, in his German translation of the Bible. Other Protestant Reformers followed his lead, so that Protestantism's Old Testament conforms to the Jewish canon but differs slightly from the Roman Catholic and Eastern Orthodox canon.

Luther advocated a married clergy, for he was no longer bound to Roman Catholicism's belief regarding the mutually exclusive nature of marriage and ordination. As the Lutheran Reformation progressed, Saxony's monasteries and convents closed. Luther helped the nuns find husbands. To set a good example, he married one himself—Katherine von Bora. They had three sons and three daughters. Theirs was a rich family life. Without doubt, the Protestant parsonage was one of the greatest gifts to emerge from the Lutheran Reformation.[2]

Another of Luther's changes was in the number of sacraments. Catholicism and Orthodoxy had seven, but Luther accepted only baptism and Holy Communion.

Brave Heart

Luther's life alternated between the tedium of his study and moments of high drama. He excelled in debates and used this forum to advance ideas and win followers to his cause. When the early Reformation forced a crisis upon Germany, Luther was forced to defend his ideas before Charles V, the Holy Roman Emperor, and the German Diet (Parliament). Told finally to recant, Luther refused, crying: "Here I stand. I can do no other, so help me God." The emperor issued a warrant for Luther's arrest, and he lived under its threat throughout his life. But Luther had the confidence of many German princes, including his own, Frederick of Saxony, who protected him.

Fortunately for Luther, the Turks invaded Austria at this time, and Charles V devoted the next 10 years to defending Europe from their threat. By the time the Turks were pushed out, the Lutheran Reformation was firmly established in many parts of Germany. Luther remarked to associates that while he and his friends sat in the garden drinking German beer, the Word of God went forth reforming the church. The point was clear: Luther worked diligently for the Reformation cause, but its success was God's work, not Luther's.

Pietism

A century after Luther, some pastors argued that Lutheranism's full potential had not been realized fully. They believed that the reform of doctrine and worship needed to be followed by a further reform of Protestant spirituality. The movement to connect church doctrine more fully with spiritual life is called Pietism. The early leaders of German Pietism were Philipp Jakob Spener and Auguste H. Francke. Pastor Spener formed circles of earnest disciples who met for Bible study and prayer. The members spoke of justification by faith in personal terms and were accountable to one another as disciples. This experiment revived Spener's churches, and his methods were adopted by others. Under the influence of his disciple Francke, the University of Halle became a leading disseminator of pietist methods and spirituality. Nicholas von Zinzendorf, educated at Halle, founded the Moravians, a pietist sect that influenced John Wesley. Pietism affected other Protestant denominations too. Historian Ernest Stoeffler identified Pietism's main themes: a new dynamic in preaching, a renewal of pastoral care, devotional life and literature, an interest in missions, social outreach, and an emphasis on discipleship.[3]

Lutherans in America

Henry Muhlenburg came to America in the 1700s to pastor three Lutheran churches formed by German and Dutch immigrants. In 1748 he organized these and other Lutheran congregations into the first Lutheran synod in America. His crucial work as a pastor and organizer earned him recognition as the principal leader of Lutheranism in colonial America.

European immigration reached flood stage in the 19th century, and Lutheran immigrants set up denominations in America that reflected their national origins. New denominations were also set up according to whether the members preferred a pietist (spiritually oriented) form of Lutheranism or a more confessional (doctrine oriented) form. Pietism was the dominant expression of Lutheranism in America during most of that century.

In the past century, a once-bewildering mosaic of Lutheran denominations has slowly coalesced into fewer and fewer separate groups. By 1995 the overwhelming majority of American Lutherans were embraced within the Evangelical Lutheran Church in America (ELCA), with 5.2 million members, and the Lutheran Church—Missouri Synod, with 2.6 million. The Wisconsin Evangelical Lutheran Synod has 415,000 adherents, and several smaller Lutheran bodies exist.[4]

Missouri Synod Lutherans and Wisconsin Lutherans derive their names from their headquarters location, not because their membership is principally located in these states. Both are Fundamentalist churches with strict views of biblical inerrancy. They strongly oppose women's ordination or pastoral leadership. Wisconsin Lutherans serve Communion to their own members only, and both churches appear doctrinaire to most people of Wesleyan-Holiness persuasion.

The Evangelical Lutheran Church in America is much more diverse. It was created in 1988 through the merger of the Lutheran Church in America and the American Lutheran Church. Both merging bodies had large Scandinavian-American components. There was also a third merger partner: the Association of Evangelical Lutheran Churches, former Missouri Synod Lutherans who left that denomination in 1976 over policies of its Fundamentalist leadership. Many of the ELCA's parent groups were pietist bodies and emphasized Christian living more than doctrinal precision. The ELCA is one of America's mainline denominations, but it is located on the conservative end of that spectrum.[5]

Lutheran churches are liturgical. Their order of worship resembles the Roman Catholic mass. Luther insisted on weekly celebration of the Eucharist, but American Lutherans are more likely to do so monthly.

Lutherans number about 68 million worldwide. Nearly 100 denominations from 50 countries participate in the Lutheran World Federation, which meets every six years to witness to Lutheran unity. The federation also sponsors theological study and the translation and publication of Lutheran literature. Lutheran World Service, a department of the federation, provides emergency and relief services to tens of thousands of refugees and poor annually.[6]

Lutherans and Nazarenes Agree . . .

Nazarenes and other Wesleyans are deeply indebted to Martin Luther and his followers. Luther's new understanding of the gospel and its sturdy defense by Lutherans ever since have added an important new dimension to Christianity.

The Church of England appropriated Luther's doctrine of *justification by grace* through faith. John Wesley, a member of that church, made this doctrine one of the theological "landmarks of the Wesleyan revival."[7] This vital doctrine is a baseline in all Protestant churches. It is reflected in the Church of the Nazarene's Articles of Faith (Article IX) and in typical Nazarene preaching. New members affirm their personal experience of God's saving grace appropriated through faith when they join a Nazarene church and enter into covenant with other believing members of the congregation.

The *priesthood of believers* has also powerfully influenced Nazarene life. The American Holiness Movement never accepted the idea that the clergy were to direct everything. Indeed, the Wesleyan-Holiness Movement arose through the initial work of Methodist laywomen led by Phoebe Palmer and her sister. Many local and even state Holiness associations were led by laypersons, and lay preachers played an important role in Nazarene origins. Nazarenes continue to see the laity as ministers in their own right and include them at every level of church governance, from the local church through the General Assembly.

Lutheran *Pietism* (the movement to connect church doctrine more fully with spiritual life) has also shaped Nazarenes, though its influence was refracted through John Wesley's Anglican lens and modified by the North American environment. Pietist modes of spirituality are traditionally the primary spiritual vehicles in Nazarene life. Prayer meetings, revivals, strong missionary interests, extemporaneous prayer (rather than printed prayer), and much of the religious vocabulary of Nazarenes is rooted in historic Protestant Pietism. A host of other innovations that date to Luther shape Nazarene life, including married clergy, the Old Testament canon, and our acceptance of two sacraments.

. . . and Differ

Where do Nazarenes and Lutherans differ? First, Wesley's distinctive theology took shape 200 years after the Reformation, when some of the inherent weaknesses in Luther's theology had become more apparent. Like the Church of England's theology itself, Wesley's theology reflects themes drawn from Protestant Reformers but also from Catholic and Eastern Orthodox writers. So the Wesleyan theological reservoir is wider than Luther's was.

This is true especially in Wesley's understanding of grace as prevenient, justifying, and sanctifying. The doctrine of prevenient grace was from Catholicism, his concept of justifying grace from Luther, and his view of sanctifying grace draws on Catholic and Eastern Orthodox sources. For Luther, *faith* is what God requires of us. For Wesley, *love* wrought by faith is what God requires. The points are similar but not identical.

This difference appears in Luther's understanding of the justified Christian as one who is *simul justus et peccator* ("at once justified and a sinner"). Luther believed that through faith we appropriate God's forgiveness of sins and are justified by grace, but he saw the Christian life as a continual battle against original sin that is not won in this lifetime but only through death. So Christians, in his view, are still sinners, but they are sinners whom God counts as righteous through Christ. Sanctification is a continual process that is incomplete at death. His view is called *imputed righteousness*. Wesley, however, argued that sanctifying grace is *imparted* to the believer and that it actually changes the believer's inward disposition. The gift of salvation brings a real change, not only in our standing before God but also *in* us.

Another difference between Nazarenes and Lutherans is over the doctrine of the Lord's Supper. The Lutheran doctrine of consubstantiation is not held by any other Christian church. It is a distinctive Eucharistic doctrine that marks Lutherans from other Christians.

Worship style is another area of difference. In Lutheranism, Pietism did not displace liturgical worship but was a supplement and adjunct to it. Nazarenes, on the other hand, have brought Pietism into the sanctuary and made it their dominant mode of worship. Nazarene pietism, however, has been shaped by the camp meeting and revival tradition.

Finally, the Nazarene concept of the *general church* is quite different. When Lutherans think of their denomination, they think in national terms. Nazarenes, on the other hand, think in international terms. We see our church as a global church and strive to be world Christians.

Our debt to Lutheranism is great. But our denominational emphasis and basic understandings of scriptural doctrine have been shaped by other Christian traditions as well, particularly by Anglicanism and its Methodist offshoot. Our debt to Lutheranism is only one of our many debts.

AT A GLANCE

CALVIN'S KIN: PRESBYTERIANS AND REFORMED CHURCHES

Principal Founder and Leader

John Calvin (1509-64) is the principal father of Reformed theology. He led the Protestant Reformation in Switzerland and France. His *Institutes of the Christian Religion* form the foundations for Reformed churches today.

Core Beliefs

Total depravity
Unconditional election
Limited atonement
Irresistible grace
Perseverance of the saints

The soil in which this TULIP grows is the doctrines of the absolute sovereignty of God and predestination.

Agreement and Differences

We share with Reformed Christians beliefs in the Holy Trinity, the authority of Scripture, the priesthood of all believers, and salvation by grace. Nazarenes, however, differ with every petal of the Reformed TULIP.

Today's Reformed Christians

The main American denominations springing from Reformed roots are
• Presbyterian Church (U.S.A.), 3.7 million members
• United Church of Christ, 1.5 million members
• Reformed Church in America, 309,000 members
• Presbyterian Church in America, 268,000 members

> **"Man's chief end is to glorify God, and to enjoy Him forever."**
> —Westminster Shorter Catechism

CHAPTER 9

CALVIN'S KIN: PRESBYTERIANS AND REFORMED CHURCHES

JOHN WESLEY NAMED THE PAPER for his Methodist followers the *Arminian Magazine*. The title distinguished the *Wesleyan* Methodists from the *Calvinistic* Methodists led by George Whitefield, a colleague to whom Wesley was indebted for many things—but not his theology.

We often use the terms "Calvinism" and "Arminianism," but what do they mean? Calvinism is a system of theology that originated in Switzerland. It became one of the great Reformation traditions. It is often referred to as "Reformed theology," for John Calvin was not the first (nor the only important) theologian to shape this perspective.

Zwingli

Ulrich Zwingli (1484—1531) was Zurich's outstanding preacher when Luther's writings stirred the Reformation tempest. A proficient Greek scholar and humanist, he quickly grasped the implications of Luther's new theology but developed his own theology of the Word. Scripture's authority was his focus, not personal salvation, as it was for Luther. Zwingli arranged public debates to promote Protestant teachings. He led Zurich to purge Catholic elements gradually from its religious practices.

Zwingli emphasized the Holy Spirit as the Author of Scripture and the indispensable Guide to its interpretation. He affirmed *sola scriptura*—the principle of Scripture as the final Authority in deciding matters of faith.[1] His *Commentary on True and False Religion* (1525) showed how important the Holy Spirit was in his baptismal theology. Zwingli insisted that water baptism and Spirit baptism are both necessary to make a Christian. One may experience water baptism first and Spirit baptism later, or the order may be reversed, or they may coincide, but inner and outer baptism are both necessary, in Zwingli's opinion, for salvation.[2]

Zwingli's theology of Communion provoked his greatest public disagreement with Luther. Zwingli rejected Catholic and Lutheran versions of Christ's bodily presence in the consecrated bread and wine. When Jesus said, "This is my body, this is my blood," Zwingli understood Him to say that the bread and wine *signify* His body and blood. The words are symbolic, Zwingli said, and doctrines of Christ's bodily presence merely confuse the symbols with the things they signify. Zwingli was adamant: the Catholic mass, which reenacts the Eucharist, does not have power to forgive sins. The forgiveness of sins comes only through the unrepeatable act of Jesus' death and resurrection. The Eucharist always points back to the Cross.[3]

When a Swiss Catholic army attacked Zurich, Zwingli defended his city. He was killed in the Battle of Kappel in 1531. His dying words, reportedly, were from Socrates: "They may kill the body but not the soul."[4] His body was dismembered and burned, but Zurich's Reformation endured and spread to other Swiss cities.

John Calvin

John Calvin (1509-64) was the Reformer of Geneva. Born in France, he trained in biblical studies at Paris and other French universities. A religious conversion in about 1533 changed his life and outlook.

Calvin moved to Switzerland in 1535. His small book, *Institutes of the Christian Religion,* was published in 1536 and reappeared in larger editions throughout his lifetime. The final edition, with over 80 chapters, set forth Reformed theology's central themes.

The Presbyterian System

One of Calvin's innovations was to restructure Geneva's churches. He identified four offices that he believed Christ instituted: those of pastor, teacher, deacon, and elder. In the Genevan system, the pastors preached, met weekly to discuss the Scriptures, and instructed ministerial candidates. They also met quarterly to discipline clergy who had offended. They were all equal, without a bishop over them. Deacons cared for the poor. Teachers educated the young. Elders—12 laymen—met weekly with pastors to apply church discipline against lay offenders.

Democratic elements—the laity's participation in governance, the lack of a bishop or superintendent—marked the Geneva way. This model became the heart of the presbyterian form of church government.

The Theater of God's Glory

John Calvin adopted Luther's doctrine of justification by grace through faith and saw its truth confirmed in Scripture and his own experience. But he placed this doctrine in a larger context, namely his view of predestination. He believed that God mercifully has chosen to save certain individuals—but not others—in spite of their sins. How did he gain this understanding?

Calvin began with the majesty of Almighty God, who creates the world as the theater of His glory. God's divine glory is reflected in two arenas: nature, where God creates and sustains; and the redemptive drama, where God shows divine purity and love through the mercies of His Son, Jesus Christ.

God gives "common grace" to all, causing the sun to shine and the rain to fall on good and wicked alike. While some may feel that the natural laws governing the universe with machinelike efficiency indicate God's remoteness, Calvin saw it differently. He regarded nature's laws as signs of God's presence and action.

Common grace is given to all, but redemptive grace, Calvin thought, is offered only to some. "Predestined" is a scriptural term that Calvin understood in a distinctive way—as "predetermined" for saving grace. God chooses out of the mass of sinful and alienated humanity individuals to enjoy the benefits of Christ's atonement. They are not chosen due to any inward or outward merit, but simply to participate in God's redemptive drama. Calvin's view of predestination is linked, then, to the idea of "limited atonement"—the notion that Christ's death does not offer the possibility of salvation to all, but only to those He has preselected to save.

The drama of redemption unfolds in human history. At the final Judgment, God shows His glory and power by saving those who were elected to receive divine mercy and in justly punishing those who were not.[5]

Paul Tillich, a 20th-century theologian, noted that "it is remarkable how little Calvin had to say about the love of God. The divine glory replaces the divine love. When he speaks of the divine love, it is love toward those who are elected. The universality of the divine love is denied."[6]

And yet Calvin's doctrine of predestination actually assured his flock! It affirmed that there is a merciful God who redeems some, even though no one *deserves* divine grace. In an age riddled with superstitious belief in witchcraft and astrology, Reformed theology taught Christians that their fate did not lie in the stars nor is subject to an evil spell. Individual destiny was in the hands of God, who demonstrates justice and mercy.

Calvin pointed to specific signs of election—a love for the church, spiritual things, and right living. These indicate (but not prove) that God's grace is effective for salvation in a person's life. Those whom God elects are drawn to grace. They do not choose it; it chooses them. But it does become real. Therefore, God has appointed certain ways of making divine grace effective in the lives of the elect.

The sacraments, the Scriptures, preaching, and the living community of faith are among God's methods to bring His elect to salvation. These means prepare the chosen ones for grace and strengthen those who are given saving faith. Calvin joined other Protestant Reformers to affirm sola fide, by "faith alone," as salvation's basic principle. By faith alone the elect receive saving grace. By faith alone they continue in its promises. But this faith is a gift, given only to a few.

Can "the elect" backslide in Reformed thinking? Only in a limited sense. They can fall away from the church, but they do not lose God's saving grace. Just as a beloved child can destroy his or her life with alcohol or drugs but still be loved, so the elect can slip into sinful ways without losing God's promise of salvation. Indeed, sin is understood in Reformed theology essentially as straying from God's perfection. So Calvinists often say that we all sin daily in thought, word, and deed.

Calvin agreed with Luther and Zwingli that infants should be baptized. He argued that infant baptism was the sign of covenant relationship among Christians just as circumcision testified to covenant relationship among the Jews. One need not despair, however, if an unbaptized infant dies. If God has predestined that child for salvation, then the child is truly saved, regardless.

Calvin readily responded to those who objected that the New Testament does not mention infant baptism. The Scriptures, he said, never mention that women partook of the Lord's Supper, but who would bar them from this sacrament on an argument based on silence? No one. Then why bar infants from baptism when the argument for doing so is also based on silence? Calvin, Luther, and Zwingli all agreed that baptism relates more to the faithful covenant community than to one's individual salvation.[7]

Arminius Takes Aim

Calvin's successors took aspects of Reformed theology to new extremes. Theodore Beza embraced a view called "double predestination."

Beza reasoned that if God predestines some to salvation, then He just as surely predestines the others to damnation. Some Reformed thinkers asserted that God's decision to save and damn was the first decree, and the decision to create the world was made in order to carry out that intention.

Another group of Reformed churchmen moved in a different direction and embraced a very different understanding of salvation. It was called Arminianism, after the Dutch theologian James Arminius (ca. 1559—1609). Holland, England, and later America became the chief centers of Arminian thought.

Arminius studied with Beza in Geneva before his installation as a preacher in Amsterdam in 1587. He played an important role in establishing the Reformed Church in Holland. In 1603 he became professor of theology at Leiden University. Arminius saw himself as a faithful son of the Dutch Reformed Church in spite of the different understanding he developed on predestination and issues linked to it.

He agreed with Calvin's doctrine of total depravity, the idea that there is no merit in us that can lay a claim on God for our salvation. But Arminius argued that Christ's atonement offers salvation to every person who accepts this gift by faith. Scripture, he believed, teaches that Christ intended the benefits of His atonement to be *universal*, not *limited* as Calvin taught. They also are *conditional*—based on faith and repentance—not *unconditional* and *irresistible* as Calvin understood them to be for "God's elect."

Arminius's logic led to another conclusion: since faith is conditional, one who has accepted God's saving grace can also lose it by backsliding through severe or persistent sin. This contrasted starkly to Calvin's doctrine of the perseverance of the saints, which was grounded in his view of predestination.

Arminius had powerful Dutch supporters, but his doctrines were condemned 10 years after his death by an international council of Reformed theologians meeting in Dort, Holland. The Arminians were forced from the Dutch Reformed Church and established a separate denomination, the Remonstrant Church, which still exists in Holland.[8]

Reformed Denominations in America

The largest Reformed church in America today is the Presbyterian Church (U.S.A.), with almost 3.7 million members. It is the accumulation of at least 10 church mergers in the past 250 years.[9] Its roots lie in the first American presbytery (local association of churches), formed in

1706, and in the first American synod (regional body), which formed 10 years later.

Presbyterians divided in the 1830s into two—New School and Old School parties. New School Presbyterians were open to revivalism, while the Old School was more consistently Calvinistic. Other divisions soon appeared. The New School divided into separate Northern and Southern churches over the slavery issue, while the Old School did the same once the Civil War began.

New and Old School Presbyterians in the North eventually set their differences aside and reunited. Old School Presbyterians in the South evolved into the dominant Presbyterian church in that region. Not until 1983 did Northern and Southern Presbyterians reunite, creating the Presbyterian Church (U.S.A.).

The Reformed people nearest to America's heart are the New England Puritans, who shaped the idea of America as a haven for religious refugees. By 1800 the Puritan churches had evolved into the Congregational Church. In the 19th century, Congregationalists worked closely with Presbyterians under the Plan of Union, an agreement by which the two denominations agreed not to compete in planting churches on the frontier. Thus, they could insure that the resources of both groups were used more effectively to establish the Reformed tradition in the West. An example of this cooperation is found in the ministry of Presbyterian revivalist Charles Finney, who pastored several Congregational churches.

Outstanding Congregationalist preachers include pastor-theologians Jonathan Edwards and Horace Bushnell, abolitionist Lyman Beecher, and Beecher's son, noted pulpiteer Henry Ward Beecher.[10]

In 1961 the Congregational Church merged with the Evangelical and Reformed Church, creating the United Church of Christ. David Stowe, brother of retired Nazarene general superintendent Eugene Stowe, was a United Church of Christ missions executive. Today this denomination has 1.5 million members in the United States.[11]

Neither the Presbyterian Church (U.S.A.) nor the United Church of Christ require strict fidelity to traditional Reformed faith today. Both have members who accept 20th-century theologies. At the same time, both also have congregations, pastors, and laity who adhere to traditional versions of Reformed theology.

Two other Reformed denominations are noteworthy. The Reformed Church in America dates to the founding of a Dutch Reformed congregation in 1628 in New Amsterdam (now New York City). The denomination grew through continuing Dutch and German immigration and was greatly augmented in the 19th century. Two generations of Phineas Bresee's ancestors were married in the Dutch Reformed Church in Albany, New York. The present church name, adopted in 1867, better represented its growing German membership, but the change also reflected the Americanization of its Dutch base. The Reformed Church in America is an Evangelical body with an inclusive membership of over 309,000. Television preacher Robert Schuller is a member of this denomination. It is a charter member of the National Council of Churches and the World Council of Churches, projecting a conservative influence within these ecumenical bodies.[12]

The Presbyterian Church in America (PCA), a relative newcomer, was organized in 1973 by congregations opposed to the merger talks that created the Presbyterian Church (U.S.A.) a decade later. The PCA has an inclusive membership of 268,000. It holds a strict view of biblical inerrancy and strongly opposes women's ordination, which it views as a compromise with biblical truth. Reaction to women's ordination in the Presbyterian Church (U.S.A.) fueled the defection of conservatives from that body into the PCA during the 1980s. The Presbyterian Church in America adheres strictly to the Westminster Confession and Westminster Catechism.[13]

South Korea

A 20th-century Presbyterian success story took place in South Korea. Presbyterian missionaries were the first Protestants to arrive there in the 19th century. Today over 20 percent of South Korea's 44 million citizens are Presbyterians. They account for over half of that country's Christians and for 60 percent of its Protestants. Yim Sung Bihn, a seminary professor in Seoul, believes that the "democratic church structure coupled with a respect for elders" that is fundamental in Presbyterianism fits well with Korean culture. He notes that South Korean Baptists and Methodists have adopted Presbyterian features.[14]

Similarities . . . and Differences

John Wesley, stout foe of Calvinism, presided at a Methodist conference in 1745 that affirmed that "the truth of the gospel lie[s] very near . . . to Calvinism . . . within a hair's breadth." What on earth did they mean?

Wesley and his associates listed three fundamental points where Calvinists were right: (1) in "ascribing all good to the free grace of God," (2) in denying that people have a *natural* free will to choose the gospel, and (3) in denying that humans have any natural merit that saves us; rather, the good we do is a response to God's grace, not a claim upon it.[15]

What about this matter of denying that we have "a natural free will"? Do we not choose to be Christians? Indeed. But Wesleyan theology asserts that our ability to choose God is a *gracious* ability—given by God through prevenient grace—and not a natural ability. Our natural free will was marred by sin, but God graciously restores our ability to respond to the gospel. Wesley's (and our) argument with Calvinism turns not on whether free will is natural or gracious, but on whether God's gift of gracious ability extends to all or only to a preselected few. Traditional Calvinists say only to a few. We say to everyone.

There are other fundamental points where Wesley—and Nazarenes—agree with the Reformed tradition: on Scripture as the primary authority for deciding doctrine *(sola scriptura)*; on the reality of original sin, which strips us of any claim upon God for salvation based upon merit; and faith in Christ as God's design for communicating saving grace. We, like Wesley, also tend to agree with Calvin's "third use of the law"—its ability to shape and inform Christian discipleship.

Our critical differences emerge around a cluster of doctrines linked to grace and election. Like Arminius, we believe that

• Christ's atonement was for all (not just a few).
• Salvation is conditional on faith and repentance (not unconditional for those who are elect).
• God's gracious offer of salvation can be resisted (not irresistible for the elect).
• Saving grace can be lost by severe or persistent sin.

Other critical differences with Calvinism are related to what Wesley brought to our theology over a century after Arminius. Among them:

• Prevenient grace drawing us toward salvation
• Sanctification as God's inward work that begins in the new birth (regeneration) and leads, through His grace, to entire sanctification of our heart
• Faith as the method by which God sanctifies the heart (not by works, and not by separation from the body)

Another basic difference: Reformed churches view their presbyterian government as scriptural. It has theological, not just organizational, meaning to them. We deny that Scripture teaches a particular pattern of church organization. Our polity combines principles and pragmatism in carrying out our mission. Nazarene government uses episcopal, presbyterian, and congregational elements alike. Our assemblies, derived from the Methodist conference system, show elements of presbyterian influence on Methodism and on us. So, too, does our practice of electing ministerial candidates to elder's orders at district assembly and inviting ordained elders to participate in the laying on of hands for new ministers. The Reformed tradition has played a critical role in Protestant development and has contributed elements to Nazarene practice and belief. But fundamental differences over the way of salvation and Christian holiness place us altogether in another category.

AT A GLANCE

CATHOLIC AND REFORMED: THE ANGLICAN PARADOX

Historical Roots

The roots of the Church of England (Anglican) reach deeply into Christian history. Its spirituality is grounded in the Celtic saints. Anglicanism broke from the Catholic Church over Henry VIII's desire for a male heir. When Rome refused his request to divorce his wife, he took English Christians out of the Catholic Church. Anglicanism's Protestant spirit is rooted in John Wycliffe and the thirst for church reform. Its theology and worship roots are in the thought and liturgy of Thomas Cranmer.

Core Beliefs

A Protestant view of the authority of Scripture.

Belief in the Apostles' and Nicene Creeds.

The practice of liturgical worship. The Thirty-nine Articles of Religion.

The *Book of Common Prayer* shows that worship is the central concern of this church.

Agreement and Differences

The Nazarene tradition is more directly influenced by the Anglican Reformation than by Luther or Calvin. Our spiritual ancestor John Wesley was an Anglican priest all his life. Our Articles of Faith, originally formulated by Phineas F. Bresee, bear the influence of the Twenty-five Articles of Religion of the Methodist Episcopal Church, which John Wesley extracted from Anglicanism's Thirty-nine Articles of Religion. Our Articles of Faith on original sin, the Trinity, Christ, justification by faith, the sacraments, and the Bible sound like the Anglican creed.

We worship differently. Though Wesley found the seeds for his doctrine of holiness in the Anglican creeds, the way we think about the holy life is different from Anglican thinking. The range of Anglican beliefs is broader than Nazarene beliefs, which stay close to Wesleyan-Arminian teachings.

Today's North American Anglicans

The Episcopal Church is the biggest Anglican church in the United States, with 2.5 million members. The Anglican Church in Canada has 850,000 members. There are several smaller Anglican groups as well.

CHAPTER 10

CATHOLIC AND REFORMED: THE ANGLICAN PARADOX

ANGLICANISM IS A WORLDWIDE COMMUNION of churches that trace their origin to the Church of England. The English Reformation began slowly under Henry VIII and accelerated under his son Edward. Catholic and Protestant martyrs alike were created before Anglicans found their niche. The Church of England became the church of the via media (middle way)—Catholic *and* Reformed.

John Wycliffe

An Oxford scholar named John Wycliffe (d. 1384) emerged as a champion of church reform over a century before the Protestant Reformation. His followers, called Lollards, were university men who popularized his ideas among ordinary folks. Wycliffe's principles included
- translating the Bible into the language of the people;
- affirming Scripture as the highest Authority in matters of doctrine;
- the predestination of the elect to grace, meaning that God (not the Catholic sacramental system) determines who is saved and damned;
- restricting the papacy;
- emphasizing preaching as a greater means of grace than the Eucharist;
- simplicity as a key characteristic of apostolic character.

His disciples paid dearly for their reforming principles. Nearly all lost academic positions, and some were burned as heretics. But they made an impact on England. Wycliffe's ideas soon spread through Europe.

The Reformation

Anglicanism originated in Henry VIII's desire to divorce his first wife after secretly marrying a second in the hope of producing a male heir. The pope refused to grant a divorce, and Parliament at Henry's instigation severed the Church in England from the Roman Catholic Church. The pope's authority over the English church was then divided between the monarch and the archbishop of Canterbury.

At first the English Reformation was limited to reforming church government, abolishing monasteries and convents, and confiscating monastic lands and other assets for the crown. Henry harbored many Catholic sympathies but had his son educated by Protestants. Moreover, Thomas Cranmer, archbishop of Canterbury, was much farther down the Protestant road in his thinking.

Cranmer made secret plans to reform Anglican worship and theology after Henry's death. Henry opposed clergy marriage; Cranmer secretly had a Lutheran wife he had married in Germany. However, his theology leaned toward Calvinism.

Cranmer's greatest achievement was the *Book of Common Prayer*, introduced in 1549 and later revised. Cranmer wrote it in such a way that those of different persuasions could find it meaningful. It contained prayer services for morning and evening worship, Sunday services, and services for holy days.

Logic of the Via Media

What does it mean when a church is both Catholic and Reformed? How did Cranmer and others see their church?

- They saw the Church of England as a church with roots in primitive Christianity.
- The Scriptures were worked thoroughly into Anglican worship—more so than in any other branch of Christianity.
- They embraced the Early Church fathers, the first commentators on Scripture, who shaped the doctrines of the Trinity and Christ's nature and defined the New Testament canon of Scripture.
- The Catholicism of the church fathers was regarded as more basic and universal than that of Roman Catholicism with its claim of papal supremacy. Anglicans saw themselves as full participants in a Catholic tradition much broader than that of Rome.
- The episcopacy (or church with bishops) was an important bulwark against heresy in early Christianity. Anglicans retained bishops as another point of identity with primitive Christianity.

The Anglican Reformers did not fully repudiate their medieval heritage. They rejected Roman Catholic additions, such as papal authority, to the broad Catholic tradition. But they did not throw out everything that was medieval.

At the same time, the Anglican Reformers
- embraced the Reformation doctrine of justification by faith;
- rejected Roman Catholic views of the sacraments, especially transubstantiation;
- affirmed scriptural authority in matters of church doctrine.

They were Protestant in another sense. Monasteries and convents were closed, so the English church after Henry had a different spiritual feeling to it than that of the Middle Ages.

A Diverse Tradition

Three religious movements have shaped Anglicanism since the Reformation: Evangelicalism, Anglo-Catholicism, and liberal theology. *Religion of the Heart.* The Church of England's Evangelical party grew out of the 18th century's Evangelical Revival. That revival involved two sets of leaders and two theologies. The Arminian Methodists, led by the Wesleys, became a separate denomination. The Calvinistic Methodists, led by George Whitefield, remained in the state church. Whitefield was also an important figure in America's Great Awakening. He traveled to America several times and established an orphanage in Georgia. Sometimes on good terms with the Wesleys and sometimes estranged (usually over theology), Whitefield combined social compassion with fervent revivalism. William Wilberforce, a second-generation Evangelical, led the fight against slavery in the British Empire.

Anglo-Catholicism. The mid-19th-century Oxford Movement led by John Henry Newman and Edward Pusey had two main objectives. One was to recover an understanding of the church as an entity independent of the state. This was done by emphasizing its Catholic character and its spiritual basis in the gospel. The other objective was to uncover the roots of Christian worship in Hebrew religion (Pusey's specialty) and the first Christian centuries (Newman's specialty). Their work led to a revival of liturgical worship. But it also led to a romanticized view of the medieval church and a critical stance toward the Protestant Reformers. Newman eventually converted to Roman Catholicism, but Anglo-Catholicism's influence continues.

Liberal Theology. A liberal theology also began emerging in the 19th century. Its many roots included new social theories, Darwinism and the new sciences, and higher criticism of the Bible.

J. Frederick Denison Maurice (1805-72) shaped theology's new mood. Raised a Unitarian, Maurice converted to a Trinitarian view of God. He became an Anglican priest and theologian. He saw Christ as the true Head of the human race who reconstitutes humanity through

His atonement. Sin, for Maurice, was a failure to understand *who* and *what* we are in relation to Christ. It is confusion about our true identities. Conversion may be dramatic or not, but it always involves a new and penetrating clarity about our relation to Christ and others.

Maurice advocated Christian socialism. His view of history was thoroughly Christian and contradicted Karl Marx's dialectical materialism. The impetus for Christian social responsibility, Maurice asserted, arises out of Christ's self-giving to us. Maurice helped found a working-man's college in London so ordinary workers could gain some education. He was also the first Anglican theologian to deny in his writings the doctrine of the everlasting punishment of the wicked. He argued that "eternal punishment" was a quality of punishment, not a length of time.[1]

Episcopalians

American Anglicanism dates to the early British settlement at Jamestown, Virginia (1607). By 1775 the Church of England had been established by law in many American colonies, including all those in the South.

The colonists were under the bishop of London. With no bishop on American soil to ordain clergy, ministerial candidates traveled to England for ordination. English priests were also sent to assist them, but never enough to overcome the chronic shortage. The situation worsened when English priests fled during the American Revolution. Those remaining were stretched to the limit, preaching and providing the sacraments to corners far removed from their regular parishes.

American independence wrought change. Thomas Jefferson's statute on religious liberty became part of Virginia's constitution and disestablished Anglicanism there. Other states adopted a similar measure, as did the federal government.

Further change came when the Methodists withdrew in 1784 to organize the Methodist Episcopal Church. Five more years passed before the remaining Anglicans organized the Protestant Episcopal Church, commonly known as The Episcopal Church. Who can gauge the loss of the Methodists for Episcopalians? In 1775 Anglicanism was the third largest denomination in America, and the Methodist societies were quite small; by 1850 the Methodists were the largest denomination in America, while the Episcopalians were fifth.

The Episcopal Church, Anglicanism's primary expression in the United States, has an inclusive membership of 2.5 million. Its General Convention is divided into a House of Bishops and House of Deputies. The latter is composed of equal numbers of elected lay and clergy delegates. Legislation must pass both houses, though on some issues separate votes by clergy and laity are required. The Anglican Church in Canada is that country's principal Anglican denomination and has a membership of about 850,000.[2]

Although Episcopalians have a reputation for liberal tolerance, the first women priests were not ordained in the United States until the 1970s, and the same did not occur in the Church of England until the mid-1990s. The strongest opposition to the ordination of women has come not from Evangelical Anglicans, but from Anglo-Catholics, a number of whom have united with the Roman Catholic Church as a result. In the United States several Anglo-Catholic denominations splintered off from the Episcopal Church over the women's issue and changes in the 1928 Prayer Book. None of the recent splinter groups are very strong, nor have any two been able to come together.

Anglican Writers

The Anglican spiritual tradition is not limited to the *Book of Common Prayer*. It is also evident in several writers who have influenced contemporary Christianity, including C. S. Lewis, Evelyn Underhill, Dorothy Sayers, and William Barclay. Underhill specialized in devotional literature, and her study of Christian mysticism reflected deep personal interests. Lewis's fiction and nonfiction works have been popular since the 1960s, including *The Chronicles of Narnia* series for children. Sayers, a novelist, used fiction (including detective stories) to explore spiritual matters. Barclay's Daily Study Bible commentaries for laypeople grew out of a radio show in which he responded to hundreds of questions about the Bible and its role in Christian life.

Anglican Distinctives

What distinguishes Anglicans? The Thirty-nine Articles of Religion have been interpreted widely by Calvinists and Arminians, Evangelicals and Anglo-Catholics. Anglicanism's focus, therefore, lies elsewhere, and that is in the *Book of Common Prayer*. Anglicans do not unite around a creed so much as around the reality of the Church as the worshiping people of God.

The *Book of Common Prayer* contains a format for different worship services—Sunday worship, holy days, and morning and evening prayer. It also contains devotional material. Scripture is liberally sprinkled throughout these services, and the book is suitable for family and private worship.

Bishop Stephen Neill identifies other characteristics of Anglicanism:

- *Biblical quality.* This is expressed in creeds and liturgy, and Neill insists that "the Anglican Churches read more of the Bible to the faithful [during worship] than any other group of Churches," and Anglican laity are urged to read the Scriptures in their homes as well.[3]
- *Liturgical.* Members are expected to attend worship regularly and partake of the Eucharist. The aim of liturgical worship "is not that of producing immediate emotional results, but of gradually building up a settled resolute will to holiness, based more on the direction of the will than on the stirring of the emotions."[4]
- *Continuity.* Anglicans embrace their Celtic, Catholic, and Protestant roots. They have a keen sense of belonging to the Church Universal.
- *Episcopacy.* The episcopacy is viewed as an apostolic link to early Christianity and as a tie to the Church in all ages.
- *Saintliness.* A life of holiness is affirmed, although Anglicans understand its moral dimensions and obligations differently than Nazarenes do. The strong spiritual core at the base of Anglican life is reflected in the *Book of Common Prayer.*[5]
- *Comprehensive,* or inclusive. In the Church of England, this takes the form of gathering all the different segments of the English people into one church. "Is it not desirable," Neill asks, "that, among those who are agreed on the fundamentals of the Christian faith, there should be a measure of latitude in interpretation?"[6]

Anglican Influences

The doctrinal statements in the Nazarene *Manual* are closer to the Thirty-nine Articles than to any other Reformation creed. The reason is simple: Phineas F. Bresee prepared Articles of Faith for our church that were adapted from the Twenty-five Articles of Religion of the Methodist Episcopal Church. John Wesley, in turn, had adapted those from the Thirty-nine Articles. A line of descent marks our doctrinal lineage. It can even be traced in specific phrases in our *Manual,* such as those on original sin.[7] Note the similarities in the following:

Thirty-nine Articles (Church of England)

"Original sin . . . is the fault and corruption of the nature of every man, that naturally is engendered of the offspring of Adam, whereby man is very far gone from original righteousness, and is of his own nature inclined to evil, so that the flesh lusteth always contrary to the Spirit."

Twenty-five Articles (Methodist)

"Original sin . . . is the corruption of the nature of every man, that naturally is engendered of the offspring of Adam, whereby man is very far gone from original righteousness, and of his own nature inclined to evil, and that continually."

Nazarene Manual, 1908

"Original Sin is that corruption of the nature of all who are engendered as the offspring of Adam, whereby everyone is very far gone from original righteousness, and is inclined to evil, and that continually."

Nazarene Manual, 1997

"We believe that original sin, or depravity, is that corruption of the nature of all the offspring of Adam by reason of which everyone is very far gone from original righteousness . . . and inclined to evil, and that continually."

Anglican roots of Nazarene belief are evident in other doctrines, sometimes in identical phrases, sometimes in their general thrust, including those on

- the triune nature of God,
- the work of Christ,
- justification by faith alone,
- the Scriptures,
- baptism and the Lord's Supper (including the precise term "Lord's Supper"),
- free will as God's gracious gift, not our natural ability.

There are other linkages as well.

Our Wesleyan theology of salvation. The Wesleyan theology of salvation parallels the principle of the via media. Wesley married the Protestant emphasis on justification by faith with the Catholic (and Eastern Orthodox) emphasis on saintliness, or holiness. He understood more thoroughly than Catholic and Protestant predecessors that the faith that justifies the Christian generates evangelical love, or holiness, and that faith and love form an indivisible unity.

The doctrine of Scripture. The Church of England's Article VI, titled "Of the Sufficiency of the Holy Scriptures for Salvation," dates back to the Protestant Reformation. "Sufficiency of Scripture" means that the Bible is the definite Guide to salvation, and that anything not found in the Bible cannot be imposed as an article of faith or considered necessary for salvation. John Wesley carried this doctrine over into Methodism's Articles of Religion, and it was taught through the Methodist course of study to our Nazarene founders of Methodist background.

What essential differences separate Anglicanism and the Church of the Nazarene? They fall in three broad areas: doctrine, worship, and latitude.

Doctrine. The Nazarene *Manual* contains specific articles of faith that represent the heart of Wesleyan theology. These include statements on

- repentance,
- new birth (regeneration) and adoption by God,
- entire sanctification.

These are doctrines of spiritual life that were influenced by Pietism and took definite shape in John Wesley's theology. They are not necessarily inconsistent with Anglicanism, but neither are they specified there. We *do* specify them, and they distinguish us and our kin in the Wesleyan-Holiness tradition from other churches that came before us.

Worship. The *Book of Common Prayer* specifies an order of worship for various occasions, but very little is specified in Nazarene worship. Our worship traditions have been shaped by the camp meeting, prayer meeting, revival, and evangelistic crusade. Public testimony, extemporaneous prayer, and kneeling at the altar rail in response to an invitation to receive Christ or press on to Christian perfection are aspects of a very different worship tradition. The typical Sunday morning service of worship in the Church of the Nazarene reflects the personality and instincts of a particular pastor and people, not the cadences of the *Book of Common Prayer*.

Degree and type of doctrinal latitude. The doctrines of Anglicanism have been affirmed by radically diverse groups, and that high degree of diversity seems unlikely in the Church of the Nazarene. Our Articles of Faith provide less "elbow room" and are oriented in a definite Protestant, Arminian, and Wesleyan direction. Nevertheless, the extent of this difference is less than it was a generation ago as Nazarenes' participation in parachurch movements with Calvinistic and Pentecostal biases are reshaping popular thinking in the church.

The Anglican tradition is important in Christian history and to Nazarenes. Our lineage splits off with the decision of American Methodists to form a separate church. Nevertheless, it is through our Anglican roots that we are oriented most strongly toward the Protestant Reformation and to the Christian Church before the Reformation.

PART 5

THE TRADITION OF THE BELIEVERS' CHURCH

AT A GLANCE

THE PEACE CHURCHES: ANABAPTISTS, BRETHREN, AND QUAKERS

Historical Roots

Anabaptists are rooted in the radical religious ferment of early-16th-century Europe. The complex movement sought a believers' church free from state interference. Many early Anabaptists were burned, hanged, or drowned. Menno Simons, from whom the Mennonites took their name, was the best-known leader.

The Church of the Brethren was founded in 1708 by Alexander Mack in Schwarzenau, Germany. They blended the Anabaptist view of the church with German Pietism, or holiness of heart and life.

The Quakers, founded by George Fox, taught by Robert Barclay, and led in America by William Penn, came into existence in England about the same time that the Wesleyan revival was occurring. The teaching of the "inner light" as revelation of God distinguishes the Quakers.

Core Beliefs

1. Christian pacifism—refusal to participate in war—characterizes nearly all peace churches even today.
2. Complete separation of church and state.
3. Adult believer baptism rather than infant baptism. (The Quakers believe, however, only in the baptism of the Spirit.)
4. Holy living, shunning worldliness, and a personal relationship with God.
5. Church discipline of backsliders.

Agreement and Differences

The Nazarenes share several similar beliefs and practices, including a believers' church, redemptive social action, and the emphasis on discipleship and church discipline.

We disagree with the Quakers' spiritualizing of the sacraments. While we respect the peace witness of the pacifist churches, we do not require our members to refuse military service.

Peace Churches Today

Contemporary Anabaptist churches include the Mennonite Church, General Conference Mennonite Church, Mennonite Brethren, Old Order Amish Church, and the Hutterite Brethren. Altogether, these groups have some 335,000 adherents in North America.

The Brethren organized in America on Christmas 1723. Now seven Brethren denominations have 256,000 members.

North American Quakers make up three denominations numbering about 124,000. A number of early Nazarene leaders had Quaker backgrounds.

CHAPTER 11

THE PEACE CHURCHES: ANABAPTISTS, BRETHREN, AND QUAKERS

IT'S HARD TO THINK OF A QUAINT AMISH COUPLE, riding in their horse-drawn buggy, as martyrs. What connection could they have to a pious German woman of another century, strapped to a ladder laid across a fire? Or what connection could there be between a congregation of 18th-century London Quakers—their hour-long worship service punctuated by few words—and a relief worker feeding the starving in Bangladesh?

Quite a lot, as it turns out.

The Sermon on the Mount holds a special place in the theology and ethics of three families of churches: Anabaptists, Brethren, and Quakers. Generally, these groups reject the idea that Christians should participate in warfare. In the 20th century, their "peace witness" has led them into ministries of reconciliation, social justice, and worldwide networks of voluntary social service.

These groups are linked to another big idea that has exercised a powerful influence on modern Protestantism: the concept of the believers' church. The 16th-century Anabaptists were the modern pioneers of this theory. They rejected the legitimacy of official state churches, arguing that God's visible Church on earth is composed only of those who testify to being regenerated and who voluntarily associate together. Quakers, Baptists, and Brethren emerged in subsequent centuries as faith traditions that also strongly embraced the believers' church concept.

While believers' churches are small in Europe and South America, where state churches still predominate, they are the dominant pattern of Christianity in North America, Africa, and Asia. The influence of Quakers in Pennsylvania, Delaware, and New Jersey, and Baptists in Rhode Island, made these places laboratories of religious freedom that influenced the ideals of the new American nation. Thus, the believers' church emphasis of these "peace churches" has given them greater influence on other religious groups than many realize.

The Radical Reformation

The Anabaptist movement was part of the "radical Reformation." The radical Reformation was not a cohesive wing like the Lutheran and Reformed wings. The radical wing included Socinians, precursors of modern Unitarianism, and Spiritualists, who believed that all church organizations were fallen and sinful. To Spiritualists, the only church that counted was the "invisible Church" of true believers known only in God's heart and mind.

By contrast, Anabaptists joyfully embraced the idea of the visible Church in the world. But they sought to rescue the Church from those who linked it to the state's power. They believed that Roman Emperor Constantine's embrace of Christianity in the early fourth century was fatal for Christianity's spiritual health. From that point on, they believed, secular rulers had corrupted the religion of "the Powerless One" sent by God to save the world. Anabaptists saw this as a major flaw in Eastern Orthodoxy, Roman Catholicism, and the major branches of the Reformation.

"Anabaptist" means "rebaptized one." Everyone baptized as infants had to be rebaptized the first time they joined an Anabaptist congregation. Why? Because Anabaptists placed the highest importance on the holiness and integrity of the visible Church. Since baptism signifies incorporation into Christ's Church, they reasoned that it should be administered to those who show adult repentance and give evidence of regeneration. When their own children were born, they did not baptize them, as the Lutherans and Presbyterians did. They waited for their children to make their own public profession of faith.

These ideas of the Church and sacraments set Anabaptists apart from other churches of their day.

Anabaptist Origins

Anabaptism developed simultaneously in several parts of Europe. Why were Anabaptists persecuted by Catholics and Protestants alike? One reason is that the movement developed in a time of social turmoil. The Peasants' Revolt in Germany (1524-25) was a climactic moment of class struggle. Anabaptism appealed to the poor and socially disenfranchised, and any movement that did so was regarded with suspicion by authorities.

Moreover, if the poor opted out of the state church while the wealthy did not, this would undercut the religious unity that princes usually enforced to help maintain social stability. The teaching that Christians should not participate in combat was also viewed with alarm. Rulers need soldiers to advance their aims. Roman Catholics tended to execute Anabaptist leaders for heresy. Protestants executed them for sedition.

Anabaptist Distinctives

The seven Articles of Religion that Michael Sattler presented in 1527 to the Anabaptist conference in Schleitheim, Switzerland, form the key document of early Anabaptist belief. The articles state the following:

- Baptism can be administered only to those who have repented and truly believe that Christ has taken away their sins, and accordingly have amended their lives.
- Church discipline is to be applied to those who backslide. They are to be dealt with privately, and if that does not lead to correction, they should be banned publicly before the congregation partakes of the Lord's Supper.
- The Lord's Supper is reserved only for those in the covenant community.
- Believers are to be separated from sin and evil. Worldliness is to be shunned.
- The "shepherd in the church" (pastor) must be a person of good character, chosen by the congregation.
- Members of "the flock" are to refrain from holding government office or from helping government officials wield "the sword" of secular power. God has instituted secular power to control evildoers. But Christians live by a higher law of love.
- Christians are not to swear oaths. Instead, their character is to be so high that swearing an oath would not add one whit to their credibility, for their yes always means yes, and their no always means no.[1]

The distinctive themes are clear: separation from the world, including the exercise of secular power; repentance; amendment of one's life; baptism as a sign of repentance and affiliation with the community of faith; and the church as a righteous, or holy, community.

While not every early Anabaptist was a pacifist, the Schleitheim principles were adopted by the movement's third generation, and they came to characterize all the Anabaptist groups that endured.

American Denominations

Dutch Mennonites eventually experienced toleration. But those in German states were constantly subject to military service. In the 1700s many moved to Pennsylvania. Still others emigrated to Russia at Catherine the Great's invitation, living there prosperously for several generations and blending German and Russian cultures. After 1880, many of the Russian Mennonites went to America.

The *Mennonite Church* was organized in colonial Pennsylvania. One of the earliest appeals against slavery by a religious group was issued by the Germantown, Pennsylvania, Mennonite congregation. The Russian immigrants who later settled on farms on the Great Plains and western Canada tended to join a Mennonite Church offshoot, the *General Conference Mennonite Church*. Nearly half of its members live in Canada. The two denominations have committed themselves to a merger that should unite over 160,000 believers by the year 2000. The doctrinal basis for their merger is a new confession of faith titled "A Confession of Faith in a Mennonite Perspective."

Other Russian immigrants formed the *Mennonite Brethren* church. Unlike traditional Anabaptists, Mennonite Brethren practice revivalism and reflect the impact of the pietist movement on Mennonite communities in Russia. There are 50,000 Mennonite Brethren in North America, the majority living in Canada.

The *Old Order Amish Church* is the most conservative branch of Mennonites. Followers of Bishop Jacob Ammann, they separated from other Mennonite bodies in 1693, migrating to America in the 1700s. Theirs is a network of house churches, each with a bishop and two other clergy chosen by lot to serve for life. To preserve themselves from cultural influences that they deem harmful, the Amish have built a cultural wall between themselves and the outside world, rejecting certain modern technologies and practices, but not others. Nearly 81,000 Amish live in the United States, and an indeterminate number are in Canada.[2]

Church of the Brethren

Nearly 200 years after the Reformation, the German Baptist Brethren emerged in Schwarzenau, Germany. They borrowed the Anabaptist view of the church and united it with the spiritual style of another movement called Pietism.

The Brethren founder was Alexander Mack, who in 1708 was rebaptized with seven others in the Eder River. Like other pietists, they taught the need of "awakening" to one's sinful condition and experiencing "the new birth." They conducted prayer meetings. Pietists such as

John Wesley created discipleship groups within the state churches. But the Brethren insisted on a church free of state connections, marked by believers' baptism, a confession of personal faith in Christ as a condition for church membership, and the application of church discipline to backsliders. Like the Anabaptists, Brethren also embraced Christian pacifism.

Two aspects of the Brethren doctrine of baptism distinguished them from Anabaptists. Brethren insisted that the New Testament teaches baptism by immersion only. And they held that immersion must be administered three times (for Father, Son, and Holy Spirit) by leaning forward, not backward, into the water. Because they "dunked" baptismal candidates, the Brethren were also known as "Dunkards" and "Tunkers."

The Brethren were persecuted for their pacifism and for their attitude toward the state church, which they insisted was fallen. Most Brethren migrated to America beginning in 1719, and they organized an American church on Christmas Day, 1723.

The emphasis on Evangelical spirit and faith, coupled with Anabaptist views of discipleship and church, provided a solid basis for Brethren unity for a century and a half. But the movement suffered a three-way split in the 1880s in the face of cultural pressures.

Ultraconservatives broke off and took the name *Old German Baptist Brethren*. They emphasize plain dress (their women wear bonnets) and maintain strong ethnic German traditions. Their 5,600 members registered a growth rate of only 20 percent in over 100 years.

The Progressive Brethren were on the other end of the spectrum. They sought to bring the Brethren up to date by adopting methods used by larger Evangelical churches. The Progressive Brethren today exist in two denominations: *The Brethren Church (Ashland, Ohio)*, with less than 14,000 members, and the *Fellowship of Grace Brethren Churches*, with about 40,000 adherents.

The great majority of Brethren were in the middle. They modernized but did so more slowly than the Progressive Brethren. Some identified with liberal Protestantism. They took the name *Church of the Brethren* in 1908 and currently have about 143,000 members in the United States.[3] The Church of the Brethren maintains a strong "peace witness," which has not been the case with the Progressive Brethren denominations.

Quakers: The Inner Light

Every theology has controlling insights—powerful ideas at the center that shape the larger point of view. The controlling insight in Quaker theology is based on John 1:9, which speaks of Christ as "the true light, which enlightens everyone" (NRSV). To George Fox, the founder of the Quakers, this verse meant that Christ's light shining in each person means that God has already established a relationship with them, making them persons of the utmost worth.

Fox preached the doctrine of the inner light throughout England in the middle part of the 17th century. His followers were called Friends, though others called them Quakers, as they were thought to "quake" in the Spirit. Robert Barclay was their prominent early theologian, and William Penn was an early convert.

What is the inner light? It cannot be identified simply with the conscience, for conscience is culturally conditioned to some extent. Only to the extent that conscience is God-shaped can it be identified with the Quaker doctrine. But the inner light is greater even than this aspect of conscience; it is a path, and if it is followed, it can lead one to a personal knowledge of God.

The inner light is a source of personal revelation of God that exists apart from the Bible. But it does not conflict with the Bible, Quakers insist, for what God reveals to you or to another will not conflict with what God revealed in other times and places. The Bible is a record of revelation, and thus a guide to all who follow the inner light today.

The doctrine of the inner light was viewed as a heresy by the Puritans, who emphasized God's revelation in Scripture. Quakers who preached in 17th-century Massachusetts were flogged and sometimes hanged. But the Quakers did not back down. They were saying that doctrine must be experienced, not simply received by the mind.

The inner light idea transformed everything about Quaker life and ethics. It completely altered the Quaker theology of the sacraments. Adherents reinterpreted baptism and the Lord's Supper in completely spiritual terms. To them the true baptism is baptism in the Spirit; true Communion is the communion of Christians through the Holy Spirit.

The inner light also stood at the center of Quaker worship. The Anglican *Book of Common Prayer* was thrown out, along with every other kind of structured service. The Quaker meeting had no agenda and no priests to lead it. Once the meeting began, all was steeped in silent prayer and meditation except when someone spoke out in song, prayer, or exhortation at the prompting of the Spirit. Even today in those Quaker churches where silent worship still prevails, it is not uncommon for there to be two or three brief "testimonies" of 5 to 10 minutes each, with the rest of the service made up of silent meditation.

The inner light affected Quaker ethics. It is a reason why they took the Sermon on the Mount with such literal application. If the inner light is within each person, how can I bear arms against another and kill that one when God has already staked a claim on his or her life? Pacifism did not free Quakers from military language, however. They talked of "the Lamb's war" that Christ wages against iniquity. They preached that weapons of forgiveness and compassion used by soldiers in the Lamb's war exceed in power the carnal weapons of destruction used by kings and emperors.

Quakers were early and fervent foes of American slavery. How can one hold in bondage a fellow human being in whom Christ's inner light is present? They were generally fair in their dealing with Native Americans and paid them for the land they used despite the fact the British monarch had "granted" that land for their use.

Quakers and Religious Liberty

Quakers were important in shaping American religious liberty. Persecuted in England, many sought a more humane life in the New World. In Delaware, Rhode Island, and New Jersey, they constituted an important social and political block that fostered toleration of religious minorities. Their influence was greatest in Pennsylvania, however, which was transferred by the English king to William Penn to settle a debt. There they established what they hoped would be a model government for the world. They dominated the colonial legislature for several generations.

This illustrates a point: unlike Mennonites and Brethren, Quakers were involved in government affairs. Ironically, their attempts at a model government ended in the mid-1700s, when the governor of Pennsylvania, appointed by the king, issued a bounty for the scalp of any Native American, regardless of gender or age. The Quakers resigned from the legislature in horror and protest and were succeeded by men whose principles were quite different.

The way in which the Quaker experiment in Pennsylvania ended discouraged many Friends. But the *Journal of John Woolman,* a classic in American religious autobiography, begins soon after this period, as Quakers found their social purpose renewed in their witness against slavery.

Quaker Denominations

The Quaker service of worship is called the meeting, and the house of worship is "the meetinghouse." But local meetings are part of larger bodies called Yearly Meetings. The various Yearly Meetings were linked for several generations, but this changed in the 1830s.

A liberal group led by Elias Hicks moved toward a Unitarian view of God. Hicks argued that "Christ was the Son of God in the same sense that all people were." He denied traditional doctrines of Christ's atonement, original sin, and the devil. He regarded the Bible as inferior to one's immediate experience of God.[4] The Hicksites were not some small minority, and these teachings created strong dissension. By 1830 American Friends were divided, and bitterness continued between *Orthodox Friends* and Hicksites for many years. In 1900 the Hicksites organized the *Friends General Conference,* which has 31,400 members today.

Other disruptions occurred over innovations in Quaker worship and fellowship with non-Quakers. Many Quakers reacted to liberalism by moving into an Evangelical mainstream dominated by Methodists, Baptists, and Presbyterians. Joseph John Gurney, who led Quaker Evangelicals in England and America, nearly repudiated the whole idea of the inner light because his views had conformed so thoroughly to those held by other Evangelicals. The Gurneyites eventually became a majority of America's Orthodox Friends.

Some of the Gurneyites adopted the Wesleyan view of the new birth and entire sanctification and joined Holiness churches. Edgar P. Ellyson, an early Nazarene general superintendent, and his wife, Mary Emily Ellyson, came into the Church of the Nazarene from the Holiness Quakers. So, too, did Susan Fitkin, founding president of the Nazarene World Mission Society.

The other Gurneyites created their own denominational structure in 1902, known today as *Friends United Meeting.* Their United States membership is about 44,000.[5] They were influenced by modern liberal theology in the early 20th century. Rufus Jones, perhaps the leading 20th-century Quaker, emphasized the mystical aspects of Quaker theology in light of conclusions he believed had been demonstrated by modern biblical criticism.

The pattern of worship in Friends United Meeting churches is now programmed, with offering, song, and sermon. A period for silent meditation usually remains, however, as an influence from earlier days. *Conservative Friends* and Friends General Conference services typically perpetuate original Quaker worship.

Peace Church Social Witness

Jesus said that if someone strikes you on the cheek, you should turn the other cheek (Matt. 5:39). He also said, "Blessed are the peacemakers" (v. 9), and "being a peacemaker" implies being active, not passive, in the face of evil. Twentieth-century peace churches have taken seriously the mandate to be peacemakers.

The Brethren in Christ participated in founding Church World Service, an interchurch agency providing disaster relief and social services in Christ's name around the world. Quakers and Mennonites have their own networks: the American Friends Service Committee and Mennonite Central Committee. Mennonite Disaster Service is another agency that is well known for quickly getting work teams to sites where disasters have occurred. Another area where members of peace churches excel is in medicine. This is largely a by-product of serving in noncombatant roles—often in health-related fields—during times of war.

Nazarenes and the Peace Churches

Nazarenes share several vital points of interest with the peace churches. First, the Church of the Nazarene is a believers' church and makes profession of faith a condition of church membership. This characteristic is directly inherited from the Anabaptist heritage. Nazarenes in America are indebted further for the way the peace churches fostered an atmosphere in which believers' churches could thrive during an early and critical time in American history.

Nazarenes share with the peace church an emphasis on discipleship. This common thread is expressed both in the individual's personal journey with God and socially. The strong support Nazarenes give to Nazarene Compassionate Ministries indicates that we share the peace churches' desire to make a positive social witness in the name of Jesus Christ.

Beyond these general areas of agreement, we also share things with individual peace churches:

- the pietist heritage of the Brethren
- similarities between our Wesleyan doctrine of prevenient grace, in which we see God at work to some degree in every person, and the Quaker doctrine of the inner light
- the Mennonite and Brethren importance placed on the sacraments—while we disagree with the way Quakers spiritualize these tangible ways in which God presents himself to us

But the Church of the Nazarene is not a peace church in the classical sense that Friends, Mennonites, and Brethren are. We do, however, take steps to protect those Nazarenes who are conscientious objectors to military service, and we have always worked to ensure that they are accorded the same status given to conscientious objectors in other denominations.

Another difference is that the peace churches do not share our Anglican-Methodist heritage, which shapes us distinctly. Although Quakers arose in England, they repudiated Anglicanism thoroughly. Some of our doctrinal statements, on the other hand, descend from Anglicanism and tie us into that Reformation tradition. Similarly, the Wesleyan aspects of our heritage are foreign to the three peace churches, except among the Evangelical Friends.

AT A GLANCE

THE BAPTISTS:
A PRIESTHOOD OF BELIEVERS

Historical Background

The first Baptist congregation appeared near London in 1612. Roger Williams established the first Baptist church in America in 1639. The first Baptist college was the College of Rhode Island, now Brown University. Landmark Baptists, however, deny these origins, tracing their ecclesiastical existence back to Jesus himself.

Core Beliefs

Specific beliefs vary among the many Baptist congregations, but generally held Baptist doctrines include

1. autonomy of the local church,
2. ordinances rather than sacraments,
3. priesthood of all believers,
4. religious freedom,
5. soul liberty—freedom to make personal choices on matters of faith and morals,
6. baptism of adult believers by immersion only,
7. Communion for local church members only,
8. male clergy,
9. a believers' church of the regenerate only,
10. simple, vernacular worship style.

Agreement and Differences

Nazarenes share common ground with many Baptists on such points as the believers' church, priesthood of believers, and worship style. Nazarenes disagree with immersion-only baptism, all-male clergy, the Baptist view of the sacraments, and most vigorously with the predominant Baptist views of salvation, which are rooted in Calvinism. (See chapter 9.)

Nevertheless, Nazarenes have been profoundly influenced by the Baptist dominance of Evangelicalism. They have influenced us in the way we worship, baptize, regard women (in ministry and life), organize and operate Sunday Schools, and so on.

Baptists Today

The Baptist World Congress represents 191 Baptist organizations with 41.6 million members; 32.7 million are in North America. These totals do not include several Baptist denominations who do not participate in the Baptist World Congress.

Baptists you know: William Carey, Martin Luther King Jr., Walter Rauschenbusch, Charles H. Spurgeon, Billy Graham, Jimmy Carter, and Bill Clinton.

CHAPTER 12

THE BAPTISTS: A PRIESTHOOD OF BELIEVERS

THE NAME "BAPTIST" conjures many different images. What does it conjure for you? Are Baptists Calvinists or Arminians? Fundamentalists, moderate Evangelicals, or theological liberals? Are they mission-minded or antimissionary? Would they rather hold a revival or march for social justice? Do Baptists ordain women, or do they not?

If you are White and have lived in the American South, you probably would say that Baptists are Calvinists, that some are moderate Evangelicals but many are rigid Fundamentalists, that they are revivalistic and mission-minded, and they oppose the ordination of women.

But if you are one of more than 10 million African-Americans who belong to a Black Baptist denomination, your view of who Baptists are and how they think would be different. You would see the Baptists as an activist and socially responsible church. You would remember the critical role of Baptist leaders, including Martin Luther King Jr., in the civil rights struggle of the 1960s.

If you lived near the University of Chicago, founded under Baptist auspices a century ago, you might have still another image of Baptists. You would know of some who are theological and social liberals. You might even be aware of the influence of Baptist theologian Walter Rauschenbusch on the development of the social gospel's theology in the early 20th century.

Each descriptor in the first paragraph fits one Baptist group or another. That some Baptist churches are Calvinistic while others are not reflects a basic point. There is a theological core that unites all Baptists, but that core is not a particular understanding of the way of salvation.

Rather, it is a specific set of beliefs regarding the essential nature of the church and its relation to discipleship.

Here is one other question to ponder: are Baptists largely an American phenomenon, or are they a worldwide movement?

Baptist Origins

The Baptist tradition originated in England early in the reign of King James I. The Anglican Reformation was nearly 50 years old. The Church of England required its priests to use Thomas Cranmer's *Book of Common Prayer* in all public worship. And this was a problem for Puritans, a faction within the church. The *Prayer Book* was an abridgment of older Roman Catholic worship manuals, edited to reflect Protestant theology. But Puritans wanted to "purify" the Church of England of *all* Roman Catholic influences and alter the liturgy so that it conformed to the style of worship developed by John Calvin in Geneva.

Several small groups left the Church of England in the midst of the Puritan agitation. The first Baptist congregation was started, near London, in about 1612. Its founder was Thomas Helwys, and his church differed from other Separatist churches because it rejected infant baptism. Instead, they taught believers' baptism. Their doctrine of the church was similar to that of the Anabaptists. Like them, Helwys insisted on a regenerate church membership, believers' baptism, the discipline of backsliders, and the separation of church and state. But he rejected Mennonite pacifism and other ethical commitments flowing from the pacifist stance. He believed that Christians could serve in government without violating their consciences, something Mennonites did not accept. Helwys penned a booklet calling for freedom of worship and dedicated it to King James. As a result, he was imprisoned and never freed.[1]

But that first Baptist congregation endured, and by 1644 there were 47 Baptist congregations in England. They were known as General Baptists, for they held to Arminian views of God's grace, believing that Christ's atonement for sin was for everyone who would believe in Him, and that any person could be saved by grace through faith.

There was another type of Baptist church emerging by this time, however, known as Particular Baptists. The first Particular Baptist congregation was founded in about 1640. They were Calvinistic. "Particular" referred to their Calvinistic belief that Christ had not died for everyone but only for the special (particular) few God had predestined for salvation before the world began.[2]

Early Baptists in America

Roger Williams, founder of the Rhode Island colony, helped establish the first Baptist church in America at Providence in 1639. He withdrew from it a few months later. Over a century later, the College of Rhode Island (now Brown University) was established in Providence as the first Baptist college in America.

The Great Awakening of the mid-1700s stimulated Baptist growth in the Northeast. During the Awakening, some of the revived Congregationalists accepted Baptist views on believers' baptism and the strict independence of the local church. Meanwhile, Baptist life was experiencing great success in the Carolinas.

A growing Baptist witness in Virginia was also vital. After American Independence, Virginia's Baptists joined Presbyterians to lobby for Thomas Jefferson's clause on religious liberty, which was designed to separate the Anglican church from the government of the new Commonwealth of Virginia. Baptist voices helped the clause become part of the Virginia constitution, which in turn influenced the First Amendment to the Constitution of the United States.

By 1800 Baptists were poised for significant growth. As America's frontier moved ever westward, Methodists and Baptists excelled in reaching the new settlements. In 1776 Baptists claimed nearly 17 percent of all church members in America, while Methodists claimed only 2.5 percent. By 1850 Methodists had increased their share to over 34 percent and were the largest religious group in America, while Baptists cornered nearly 21 percent. How well were these churches doing? The third-largest Protestant church—Presbyterians—had less than 12 percent of America's church members.

So the 19th century was the Methodist century in some respects. But the 20th century became the significant century for Baptist growth. By 1900 Baptists and Methodists were nearly equal in numbers. Roman Catholicism had overtaken both churches to become the largest denomination in America, its numbers swelled by steady immigration from Europe, especially Ireland, Italy, and Germany. Baptists began outpacing Methodists and soon surpassed them to become the largest Protestant block in America. Baptists historically have been strongly anti-Roman Catholic, so it's possible that Baptist and Roman Catholic growth in America are linked in some way.

Baptist Associations

Baptist churches are fiercely local and independent. So how do they relate to one another? The primary way is through local, state, and national "associations" of churches, sometimes called "conventions." The first association of denomination-wide scope was spurred into existence by missionary interests. According to Baptist historian William Brackney, the plan was to devise a system of regional and local societies, which would unite in one *general society* to carry forth the one great task of missionary endeavor. The original expectation was that local or regional organizations would meet annually and the *general* or national body would meet triennially. From 1814 to 1826, this was practically the case.[3]

The Triennial Convention became a uniting force in Baptist life until 1845, when the issues of slavery and regionalism overwhelmed the Convention, just as they had done to the Methodist General Conference the year before. The slavery issue moved to the fore after Northern Baptists learned that Triennial Convention funds supported home missionaries in Texas who were slaveholders. In the uproar, the Triennial Convention divided along regional lines into two bodies: a Southern Baptist Convention and a Northern Baptist Convention.

Doctrinal Core

Several foundational principles for Baptist thought and life include
- *Autonomy,* or the belief that each local church is independent.
- The *associational principle,* in which Baptist churches participate together in areas of common witness, especially missions, Sunday Schools, home missions, and higher education.
- *Ordinances,* a term preferred in place of the word "sacraments," since most Baptists reject the idea of baptism and the Lord's Supper having a sacramental character; instead, they view the ordinances as practices required of Christians, rather than as grace-bearing events for the church.
- *Priesthood of all believers,* an important concept from the Anabaptist Reformation that is also central in Baptist life. This principle means that all Christians are ministers to one another and to the world.
- *Religious freedom* is an important idea in Baptist life, beginning with Thomas Helwys's desire to have freedom to worship in a way different from that required by English law. There is not always unanimity among Baptists on the exact place to draw the line of religious liberty, however. While many Baptists in the South support prayer in public schools, other Baptists are staunch opponents of the practice.
- *Soul liberty,* or the idea that individuals are competent to decide for themselves matters of Christian faith and morals as they study the Scriptures and are led by the Holy Spirit.[4]

Calvinist or Arminian?

The above convictions lie at the heart of all Baptist life. But these convictions, by themselves, do not answer other important questions: *Who* shall be saved? And *how* will that be accomplished?

Baptists do answer these questions as well, but not with one voice. They unite either Calvinism or Arminianism to their doctrine of the church. General Baptists, who were Arminians, were strong during much of America's colonial period. By 1800 that was changing rapidly. Particular, or Calvinistic, Baptists began to outpace General Baptists to such an extent that most Baptist churches today are Calvinistic. Some are mildly so; others are strongly so. One smaller group of Baptists who forthrightly embrace Arminianism are known today as Freewill Baptists.

Landmarkism

A new theology arose within the Baptist movement of the mid-19th century that produced great change among Baptists in the South. It was the "Old Landmark" movement, and it asserted that Baptist churches did not originate in England but were, in fact, "true churches" that exist in a thread of unbroken continuity that goes clear back to the New Testament. Indeed, Jesus himself, it was asserted, was the true Founder of the Baptist lineage.

Landmark Baptist beliefs included these:

- The belief that only Baptist churches are true churches.
- The belief that only baptism by immersion administered in a Baptist ("true") church is true baptism; immersions that took place in a non-Baptist church were called "alien immersions," while baptisms by other modes (sprinkling or pouring) were disregarded completely.
- Closed Communion, or the idea that the Lord's Supper is restricted only to members of the local church.
- Rejection of cooperative ventures with non-Landmark churches, including those with other (non-Landmark) Baptists.[5]

Landmarkism made considerable headway in the Southern Baptist Convention. However, it never captured the *whole* Southern Baptist Convention, and in the 20th century it receded within the denomination, the victim of new scholarly interest in Baptist origins.

The Central Tradition in North and South

The Triennial Convention's division over slavery in 1845 created two major Baptist denominations in America, one for the North and one for the South. Around these two major bodies smaller ones also existed: Freewill Baptists, several African-American denominations, Swedish

Baptists, and Landmark-oriented denominations. A surprisingly large number of Baptist congregations remained completely unaffiliated with any denominational body.

The American Baptist Churches in the U.S.A. After the division of 1845, Northern Baptists perpetuated the world mission legacy of the Triennial Convention through the American Baptist Missionary Union. By 1904 they were supporting 520 missionaries around the world. A stronger denominational organization was created in 1907, and the Northern Baptist Convention name was adopted. This later changed to the American Baptist Convention name, for the word "Northern" seemed increasingly inappropriate and limiting as the denomination spread into the West and even into the South. Since 1972 the denomination has been known as the American Baptist Churches in the U.S.A.

American Baptists have formed a very diverse church. Thirty-seven percent of their present membership is African-American. Other racial minorities comprise another 3 percent. Thus, it is one of the most racially heterogeneous denominations in America.

Unlike most Baptist churches, American Baptists ordain women to the ministry and are affiliated with the National Council of Churches and World Council of Churches. In 1997 they reported slightly over 1.5 million members in the United States.[6]

The Fundamentalist Fellowship, a group within the Northern Baptist Convention, withdrew from the denomination in 1947 over what it perceived as liberalism among some of the Northern Baptist missionaries. They reorganized as a denomination, and the *Conservative Baptist Association of America* was created. In 1997 it reported 200,000 members.[7]

The Southern Baptist Convention reported nearly 15.7 million members in 1997, making it the largest Protestant denomination in America today. Its reach extends into all 50 states, but the great bulk of SBC membership remains solidly in the South. In North Carolina, for instance, one in every two churchgoers attends a church aligned with the SBC. And in a way that is characteristic of few other churches, regionalism still defines much that is typical of the Southern Baptist character.

How was that "Southern" identity shaped? Largely through identification with the slave economy and the political values and structures sustaining it. The Southern preachers who developed "biblical rationales" to morally justify Black slavery were primarily Baptists who asserted that the Bible teaches that people are inherently unequal.

Further, Southern Baptists stood for secession from the Union and supported the Confederate cause without reservation. Their fortunes and identity were intertwined so strongly with a region whose religious life they dominated that its social and economic vices were also theirs.

Northern and Southern Methodists reunited in the fourth generation after the Civil War, demonstrating the moderating influences that time and perspective eventually brought to Methodist life. Most Southern Baptists, by contrast, take pride in their regional identity and would never dream of reuniting with their Northern counterparts.

Southern Baptists have made great strides in home and foreign missions through denominational programs. Indeed, from 1845 to 1907 the denominational program of the Southern Baptist Convention was actually more centralized than that of Northern Baptists. Since 1925 the Cooperative Program has linked state Baptist conventions with the Southern Baptist Convention, sustaining national programs through reliable and systematic funding directly from state conventions, rather than through individual local churches. The basic independence of the local church, however, is still protected. Congregations can withdraw from state conventions, and no decisions made by state or national conventions are binding on a local church.

Southern Baptists have been featured prominently in the news in recent years. Two of the four most recent presidents of the United States, Jimmy Carter and Bill Clinton, are lifelong Southern Baptists. Charles Stanley and other notable Southern Baptist preachers are also visible, as televised services from their local churches are aired across North America.

Dissenters from the Central Tradition

Black Baptists. While Southern Baptists were joining their hearts and minds more tightly to the economics and politics of slavery, Black Baptist churches were slowly forming in America. The earliest appeared in the South after 1775, while others appeared in Boston, New York, and Philadelphia between 1800 and 1810.

In their own churches, African-Americans experienced freedom of worship. Equally important, they chose their own leaders and supported their own religious institutions. The Black church was virtually the only sector of public life in which African-Americans had complete self-determination. By 1821 Black Baptists had sent their first missionaries overseas.

The first Baptist associations formed by African-Americans were in the North. They were not permitted to do the same in the South until after the Civil War. Several weak conventions developed out of cooperation between different associations, but these were generally weak until 1895, when the Baptist Convention of America was formed through mergers. A split in 1915, and a further split in one of those, has resulted in three dominant Black Baptist denominations today.

The National Baptist Convention, U.S.A., is the primary body to emerge from the original Baptist Convention of America, and with 8.2 million members, it is the largest African-American denomination today. Its missionary work is limited to Africa and the Bahamas. *The National Baptist Convention of America* broke off from the National Baptist Convention, U.S.A., in 1915 over a church property dispute and today has 3.5 million members.

The Progressive National Baptist Convention resulted from a split in the National Baptist Convention, U.S.A., in 1961 over democratic structures. The public issue was whether denominational leaders should serve for life or for limited terms of service. Those who insisted on limited terms formed the Progressive National Baptist Convention after their attempts to reform the mother church failed. Underneath the surface there were other differences. The two bodies approached the looming civil rights struggle in different ways, with the National Baptist Convention, U.S.A., taking a more conservative approach and the Progressive National Baptist Convention a more activist one. Civil rights leaders Jesse Jackson and the late Martin Luther King Jr. are among the denomination's noted clergy. By 1997 the church had 2.5 million members.

Freewill Baptists. Other groups besides antimission Baptists remained aloof from the Triennial Convention. Among them were Freewill Baptists, who dissented from the Calvinism characteristic of most Baptist churches in America. Thorough Arminians, Freewill Baptists affirm Christ's universal atonement. Today the National Association of Freewill Baptists has its headquarters in Tennessee and serves a constituency just under a quarter million members.[8]

Landmark Denominations. Because of their Landmark views, some Southern groups objected strongly to the cooperative program of the Southern Baptist Convention, viewing it as unscriptural. *The American Baptist Association* (25,000 members) and the *Baptist Missionary Association of America* (230,000 members) perpetuate Landmarkism.

Other Groups. The North American Baptist world has many other groups. *The Baptist General Conference* was known originally as the Swedish Baptist Church. Though small—it has just over 135,000 members—it sustains extensive missionary work around the world.[9]

The *General Association of Regular Baptist Churches* is more Fundamentalist in nature. It originated when conservatives withdrew from the Northern Baptist Convention in 1932. Its members must affirm premillennialism. Its membership is slightly over 136,000 members.[10]

Baptist Leaders

Every tradition is proud of its great preachers, and Baptists are no exception. Few 19th-century preachers were better known than Charles H. Spurgeon. During his 38-year pastorate at London's New Park Street Church, membership increased from 232 to 5,311 members. The congregation built the famous Metropolitan Tabernacle to hold the thousands who thronged to his preaching. Spurgeon was a rigid, uncompromising Calvinist and in some respects was one of the last of the Puritans.

No 20th-century Baptist is better known or loved than Billy Graham, whose evangelistic crusades have penetrated every inhabited continent. Graham's personal journey from fiery young Fundamentalist to elder statesman of Evangelical Christianity mirrors many basic changes in modern society. In the early 1950s Graham blended an anticommunistic message with his gospel of redemption. By the mid-1980s he was preaching behind the iron curtain and understood more clearly than most that great spiritual and social unrest would produce fundamental changes in Communist countries.

Martin Luther King Jr. is the best-known Baptist social leader. He embraced a theology of nonviolent activism at Boston University. This undergirded his leadership in the civil rights cause in the 1950s and 1960s. Detractors who feared the social changes he sought called him a communist. His foes reveled in tales of moral failure in his private life, yet King took a stand against the sin of racism that few of his critics had the courage or moral discernment to do.

Nazarenes and the Baptist Tradition

Baptists and Nazarenes share a number of common characteristics:
- Baptists are among the other groups (including Mennonites and Disciples of Christ) with whom Nazarenes share a common believers' church perspective and emphasize a regenerate church membership.
- The simple, Evangelical style that characterizes Nazarene worship is typical of nearly every Baptist denomination.
- The musical traditions of Baptists and Nazarenes are close, and—except for songs that are doctrinally distinctive—a large number of songs and gospel music are interchangeable.

While we agree with Baptists on some important matters, there are fundamental points of disagreement concerning doctrine and practice:

- The great majority of Baptists hold views of salvation rooted in Reformed (Calvinist) theology that Nazarenes—anchored firmly in the Wesleyan-Arminian tradition—find contrary to sound biblical interpretation. These differences include those related to our doctrines of prevenient grace, empowered free will, entire sanctification, and the assurance of the Spirit—doctrines that define who we are and how we see the world.
- The Nazarene doctrine of the ministry differs from that held by most Baptist churches. We embrace the ordination of women and celebrate their gifts of leadership in the Body of Christ. Few Baptist groups agree with our position on this.
- The Church of the Nazarene disagrees with the Baptist insistence on the necessity of believers' baptism. Instead, we permit infants to be baptized upon the request of their parents.
- Further, Baptists generally hold that immersion is the only scriptural mode of baptism. The Church of the Nazarene denies this and provides full liberty of conscience to candidates for baptism, who may choose the mode that is in accord with their personal beliefs.
- Nazarenes teach freedom from sin through entire sanctification. Most Baptist groups teach that we will always sin in word, thought, and deed every day.
- Nazarenes and other Wesleyans teach that one must maintain an ongoing relationship with God in order to be finally saved. Most Baptists believe that once one is born again, his or her sins are forgiven—past, present, and future. The person can never again be "unsaved" and is "eternally secure" regardless of present sin in daily life.

The Baptist Challenge

The Southern Baptist Convention's rise to dominance in American religion poses a challenge to Nazarenes. We have edged ever closer to the Evangelical mainstream during our 20th-century journey, but that mainstream is increasingly influenced by Baptist modes of thought and action. Some Nazarene scholars speak of the "baptistification of the Holiness Movement." Our situation differs sharply from that of the 19th century, when Methodists were the dominant Evangelical church, and Wesleyan ideas shaped a large segment of Evangelicalism. Today the sheer numbers of Baptists in America force us to take notice of their influence. The Southern Baptist Convention is the largest Protestant body in

America. It is also the largest (but by no means only) organization pro-
moting a style of Evangelical Christianity that views hierarchical relationships in church and world as scriptural and other styles as unscriptural. This influence threads its way through discussions of the role of
women in church and society, and it affects modes of governance.

Our distinctive Wesleyan-Holiness heritage makes a worthwhile
contribution to a religious world whose uncritical assumptions are popular Baptistic ones. How well will we maintain our distinctive identity
in the years ahead?

At a Glance

Unity and Simplicity:
The Christian Church
(Disciples of Christ)

Founding Fathers

Barton W. Stone fostered a revival in Cane Ridge, Kentucky, in 1801 that was a cornerstone of this church. Thomas and Alexander Campbell, Scottish Presbyterians, founded the other branch of the movement in Pennsylvania. The branches united in 1832 to form the Christian Church (Disciples of Christ).

Core Beliefs

The founders wanted to restore the New Testament Church and unify all Christians under one banner. They rejected denominationalism and accepted no creed but the Bible. "Where the Bible speaks, we speak. Where the Bible is silent, we are silent." Their beliefs include: the New Testament as the final church Authority, adult believers' baptism by immersion only, Holy Communion only for the immersed, local church autonomy, and the right to interpret the Bible for yourself.

Agreement and Differences

Nazarenes agree with the Disciples on a high view of the Bible, Jesus Christ as the one Savior, human responsibility, and the idea that all Christians are ministers. Differences include the failure of the Disciples to clearly declare belief in the triune God, in their insistence that baptism is necessary for salvation and must be by immersion, the nature of sanctification, and the importance of rules for church members.

The Restoration Movement Today

The movement to restore pure New Testament religion and unify all Christians has split into three churches. The Christian Church (Disciples of Christ) has under 1 million members. The Christian Church (Independent) has 1.2 million. The Churches of Christ have 1.7 million in the United States, 3.3 million worldwide.

CHAPTER 13

UNITY AND SIMPLICITY:
THE CHRISTIAN CHURCH
(DISCIPLES OF CHRIST)

WHERE THE BIBLE SPEAKS, we speak. Where the Bible is silent,
we are silent." "In essentials unity. In nonessentials liberty. In all things
charity."

Such noble visions launched one of the largest churches native to
American soil. The Christian Church (Disciples of Christ) was born to
march under twin banners: restoring the pure standards of the New Testament, and the union of all believers in one "Christian" church.

The Bible was to be the only authoritative Source for doctrine,
practice, and governance. *Where the Bible speaks, we speak. Where the Bible
is silent, we are silent.* What could be more ideal? What could be harder
to achieve?

One principle helped make that vision only a hope. Members of
the movement firmly believed that one of the *essentials* required for unity was the right of all Christians to interpret the Bible for themselves.
They rejected historic Christian creeds as documents that divide Christians. They also rejected interpretations of the Scriptures connected to
earlier state churches in Europe. But this principle actually made unity
harder to achieve.

Another sticking point: Disciples elevated the New Testament far
above the Old Testament. Their frontier neighbors—Methodists, Presbyterians, and Baptists—regarded the *whole* Bible as Christian Scripture
and did not take kindly to the demotion of the Ten Commandments, the
23rd psalm, and the creation stories.

Yet the dream of Christian unity was powerful. The Disciples believed that believers, sick of the dizzying array of churches hawking
their wares on the American frontier, would rally to their call to unite
under simple Bible religion. Many did.

A Look at Origins

The name of the Christian Church (Disciples of Christ) comes from two merging entities. At the dawn of the 19th century, the followers of Barton Stone in Kentucky and southern Indiana called themselves simply "Christians" or the "Christian Church." The followers of Thomas and Alexander Campbell called themselves Disciples of Christ.

Barton Stone was a Presbyterian minister when he became a pastor in Kentucky in 1796. He attended a camp meeting in Logan County, Kentucky, in 1801 and went home to start a similar meeting at his church in Cane Ridge. Preachers of every brand arrived on the scene, as did some 10,000 to 25,000 other people. The camp meeting lasted a week and would have continued except food and shelter could not be provided for so many.

The Cane Ridge revival gave Stone a vision of Christians united without sectarian doctrines or vested denominational interests. He and other preachers withdrew from the Presbyterian Synod of Kentucky and came to be known simply as "Christians." They stressed the Bible as the only Authority and declared their intention to "sink into union with the Body of Christ at large."[1] They would "preach the simple gospel" and nothing more.[2] Their preachers would learn from the Bible only, not theology books. Better, they declared, "to enter life having only one Book, than having many, to be cast into hell."[3]

Thomas and Alexander Campbell—father and son—were Scotch-Irish Presbyterians who immigrated separately to America. Thomas did so in 1807 and took a church near Pittsburgh. Besides his own flock, he encountered a different sect of Presbyterians who were "pastorless" and administered the Lord's Supper to them. For this he was deprived of his pastorate.

He moved to Washington, Pennsylvania, and created the Christian Association, announcing that he would commune with all Christians. Further, he publicly rejected his own Calvinist background and declared that Christ had died for all persons.[4]

With the "ideal of the union of all Christians flam[ing] up in his heart more brightly than ever," Campbell drew up his famous *Declaration and Address*. It affirmed that the true Church of Christ is one, and its supreme authority is the New Testament, which gives instructions that must be followed precisely. Since creeds, confessions, and articles of faith are interpretations of Scripture, they cannot be binding or used as tests of faith. His rule was "in essentials, unity; in opinion, liberty; and in all things, charity." Each local church was to be self-governing.[5]

Campbell believed that the previous 1,800 years of church history were a mistake. It was time to start over, to restore the ancient order of things. His goal was to "take up the work of Christ where the apostles had laid it down."[6]

Alexander Campbell followed his father to America a few years later and took up the cause, emerging finally as the guiding light of the movement. By the time they merged in 1832, the Campbellites and Stonites each had about 10,000 members.

Unity and Restoration

The Disciples embarked on a noble effort to unify all Christians around a simple biblical faith. The union of the two parent groups created its own tensions. There were debates over structure, missionary societies, open and closed Communion, and whether or not to serve Communion to unimmersed persons. Even calling ministers "Reverend" was a subject of debate. But by 1870 the movement had grown to 350,000.

The years took their toll. In 1906 the movement split into two. In the 1950s, another fracture took place. Today the Restoration Movement is divided into three different bodies.

The smallest of the three is the Christian Church (Disciples of Christ), a mainline denomination, liberal in theology, with a highly educated clergy. It is active in the ecumenical movement and is represented on the National Council of Churches, World Council of Churches, and the Consultation on Church Union. It has developed a denominational machinery. Today it has slightly over 929,000 followers in the United States and 4,031 churches. Like many mainline denominations, it continues to lose members.

The Churches of Christ form the largest block within the Restoration Movement. They withdrew from the Disciples in 1906. They have 1.7 million adherents in 13,000 congregations in the United States. There are another 1.6 million adherents in 75 other countries. The original teachings of the Campbells are most rigidly endorsed in this group, which clings to its own variety of Fundamentalism. Churches of Christ shun liturgical forms but expect worship to be conducted in a dignified manner. They operate 21 colleges and publish 117 periodicals.

The Christian Church (Independent) is the name used by those who broke from the mainline Disciples in the mid-20th century. This faction has nearly 1.2 million adherents in the United States. They represent the moderate voice of the Stone-Campbell movement, rejecting the liberalism of the Disciples and the Fundamentalism of the Churches of Christ. They support some 30 colleges.

The conservatives, moderates, and liberals of the restoration movement have gone their separate ways. How ironic that these categories would prove stronger than the vision of Christian unity. But let there be no doubt: each sees itself as living out the dominant values of their rich common heritage.[7]

Nazarenes and Restoration Churches

Given the pluralism and diversity among the three bodies that emerged from the Restoration Movement, it is hard to say simply what "they" believe and practice. So we will cite only a few core beliefs that tend to represent the whole group.

1. Jesus Christ, Savior and Lord. Nazarenes heartily endorse this statement from the Disciples of Christ *Design:* "We confess that Jesus is the Christ, the Son of the Living God, and proclaim him Lord and Savior of the world."[8]

2. A High View of the Authority of the Bible. Both Nazarenes and the Restorationists endorse the Protestant doctrine of *sola scriptura.* Both claim that the Bible is the final rule for faith and practice. The Restorationists tend to be more literal in invoking the Bible as the rule for churches. While recognizing that there is a promise and fulfillment factor between the Testaments, the Nazarenes view both Old and New Testaments as Christian Scripture. The Restoration tradition, however, elevates the New Testament to the real place of authority while treating the Old Testament as valuable, but secondary.

3. Human Beings Are Free and Responsible. The Holiness Movement and the Restoration Movement were born in America, where individual freedom and democracy were prized. These factors elbowed their way into the religion of both groups. This put them in opposition to the determinism of both the religious (predestination) and secular (behaviorism) varieties.

4. Missionary Minded. Both Nazarenes and all three branches of the Restoration churches make missions a priority. The Disciples of Christ supports missionaries on five continents.

5. Every Christian Is a Minister. The Christian Church's *Design* declares, "The fundamental ministry within the church is that of Jesus Christ. . . . By virtue of membership in the church, every Christian enters into the corporate ministry of God's people."[9] Nazarenes also believe that lay ministry is very important. The Nazarenes, however, from the start, had a higher view of the ordained clergy than the early Stonites and Campbellites. The Restoration churches, suspicious early of ordained preachers and church hierarchies, have now come to appreciate the value of an educated and ordained ministry. The *Design* says, "The church recognizes an order of the ministry, set apart or ordained, under God, to equip the whole people to fulfill their corporate ministry."[10]

Points of Difference

While we share much in common, there are differences between the Nazarenes and the churches of the Restoration Movement.

1. Emphasis on Sanctification. Building on a Wesleyan foundation, Nazarenes make entire sanctification their distinctive doctrine. We believe that at some point after conversion, the Christian's heart may be brought into "complete devotement" to God, cleansed from inward sin, and filled with the Holy Spirit's love and power. The Restoration churches have nothing against pure hearts or being filled with the Spirit. But they believe that all this happens at baptism. They view the gift of the Spirit as the fifth step in the formula for salvation.

2. Christian Baptism and Conversion. Nazarenes believe that baptism is an outward sign of an inward grace already received. It is a public testimony of one's experience of salvation by grace through faith and of one's intention to live the rest of life as a dedicated follower of Christ. Restorationists tend to view baptism as an integral part of the salvation formula. Without baptism no one can be saved, many believe. Typically they teach that the salvation formula is (1) affirmation of belief that Jesus is both Son of God and Savior, (2) repentance of sin, (3) baptism, (4) forgiveness granted and received, and (5) the gift of the Spirit bestowed.

Since they believe that salvation is not possible without baptism, some Restoration churches will not serve Communion to unbaptized persons. It is "baptism [that] purges all things that have diminished the life of our spirit. The old life is buried, new life is born, sins are forgiven. Baptism represents a . . . moral cleansing, a transformation of the soul, a receiving of grace."[11]

We differ with Restorationists on another point. They proclaim that immersion is the only true Christian baptism. But we say that "baptism may be administered by sprinkling, pouring, or immersion, according to the choice of the applicant."[12]

3. The Doctrine of God. "We believe . . . that . . . God is Triune in essential being, revealed as Father, Son, and Holy Spirit."[13] With this statement, the first Nazarene article of faith begins. Since they reject creeds, the Restoration Movement churches have never officially affirmed a belief in the Trinity.

They believe in God the Father. They insist, generally, on the divinity and humanity of Jesus Christ. But no doctrine of the Holy Spirit has gained dominance in the hearts of this people who so fervently believe in the right of every Christian to interpret the Bible for themselves. Barton Stone called the Holy Spirit simply "the energy of God."[14] By rejecting the early Christian creeds, Restorationists (in our view) do not have a sufficiently strong doctrine of the Trinity.

4. Rules for Church Members. Nazarenes have produced a set of General Rules and a list of Special Rules that prescribe the way the holy life should be lived. Apparently we have believed that Christians need specific guidance about such matters as divorce, abortion, lotteries, the cinema, tobacco, liquor, dancing, secret orders, and the use of sleeping pills and stimulants.

The Restorationists, on the other hand, seek to have no rule book but the Bible. D. Duane Cummins, a Disciples of Christ leader, says, "On matters of personal morality Disciples hold a deep confidence in the ability of individuals to form judgments for themselves."[15] His *Handbook for Today's Disciples* cites ethical questions such as abortion, sexual expression, divorce, and drug use. He says that when a person raises questions about such activities, the Christian Church (Disciples) "will *not* provide a systematic blueprint for your personal behavior. It *will*, however, insist that you carefully study the moral and ethical teachings of Christ and assume full moral responsibility for your personal decisions."[16]

Working Together

As we join Christians of other traditions against the common challenges of our non-Christian, postmodern culture, we need to know each other's strengths, vulnerabilities, prized heritages, and yes, the baggage that we bring to these grand and awful times. The words of John Wesley seem to fit: "Think not the bigotry of another is any excuse for your own. . . . Beware of retorting. . . . Let him have all the bigotry to himself."[17]

PART 6

THE PENTECOSTAL AND CHARISMATIC CHURCHES

At a Glance

The Pentecostals and Charismatics

Historical Overview

The Pentecostal/Charismatic landscape has six sectors:

• *Holiness Pentecostals* emerged from the American Holiness Movement.

• *"Finished Work" Pentecostals* rejected entire sanctification and broke from Holiness Pentecostals.

• *"Jesus Only," "Unitarian," or "Oneness" Pentecostals* deny the Trinity and teach that Jesus is God's name and that believers should be baptized only in Jesus' name.

• *Charismatic fellowships* exist in mainline denominations (including the Roman Catholic Church) or as nondenominational associations (such as the Full Gospel Businessmen's Association).

• *New Charismatic denominations,* such as Calvary Chapel and Vineyard Fellowship, are emerging from the Charismatic Movement.

• The fringe of independent radical churches and ministries.

Core Beliefs

All six sectors embrace the gifts of the Holy Spirit mentioned by Paul: speaking in unknown tongues; interpretation of tongues; prophecy; and healing.

Most embrace such traditional beliefs as the inspiration of the Bible, the deity of Christ, the Virgin Birth, and Christian conversion. Beliefs about baptism, baptism with the Spirit, and entire sanctification vary among Pentecostal/Charismatic groups.

Agreement and Differences

Nazarenes share orthodox Christian views with the majority of Pentecostals and Charismatics: Scriptural authority, the deity of Christ, the Virgin Birth, and the nature of Christian conversion. But Nazarenes question and challenge the views of these groups on the doctrine of the Holy Spirit and on tongues-speaking as an evidence of holiness or as a prayer language. Nazarenes reject the three works of grace taught by some branches of the movement. We firmly reject the anti-Trinitarian views of Oneness Pentecostals.

Pentecostals and Charismatics Today

Principal bodies of Pentecostals and Charismatics in North America include these groups:

• Church of God in Christ: 5.5 million members.

• Pentecostal Holiness Church: 150,000 in the United States.

• Church of God (Cleveland, Tennessee): 730,000 in North America; 4 million worldwide.

• Assemblies of God: 2.3 million in the United States; 22 million worldwide.

• International Church of the Foursquare Gospel: 224,000 in the United States; 2 million worldwide.

• Pentecostal Assemblies of the World: 1 million in the United States.

• United Pentecostal Church International: 600,000 in North America; 2.3 million worldwide.

• New Charismatic denominations such as Calvary Chapel and Vineyard Christian Fellowship are fast-growing denominations.

Q. Are tongues-speaking Pentecostals our brothers in Christ?
A. Some of them are; others are our sisters in Christ.

—William McCumber

CHAPTER 14

THE PENTECOSTALS AND CHARISMATICS

YOU ARE SEATED at an old-fashioned revival meeting in an open-air tabernacle. The sawdust trail separates you from the Pentecostal evangelist. But wait! The revivalist ridicules the doctrine of the Trinity as a crude belief in three Gods and insists that only those baptized in the name of "Jesus only" are true Christians. Now he asks if some present previously baptized "in the name of the Father, Son, and Holy Spirit" need to be rebaptized.

The scene is much different in a South Bend, Indiana, house near Notre Dame University. An eclectic group of Roman Catholics meet for informal worship: students, town folk, and several university staff and faculty members. During prayer, the soft but unmistakable murmur of "speaking in tongues" is heard from several participants.

Or imagine a large African-American church in Memphis. Loud and vibrant music has drawn the congregation to its feet more than once. Near the end of the sermon, the preacher states passionately that some present have been saved and sanctified but need to press on and receive the baptism of the Holy Spirit "with tongues."

Last, enter an Assemblies of God church in Springfield, Missouri, for a Sunday morning service. The worship differs little in style or content from that in the nearby Church of the Nazarene. Similar mix of hymns and praise choruses. Similar pastoral prayer. Similar sermon. Slight nuances of terminology, but never a sermon on—or even a mention of—entire sanctification.

Each setting represents a different aspect of Pentecostal/Charismatic religion, a world of immense diversity.

The relationship between Wesleyan-Holiness and Pentecostal/Charismatic churches often seems equally as complicated. Wesleyans have viewed Pentecostals as good folks who have "gone off the deep end," while Pentecostals (returning the favor) have viewed us as good folks who have stopped short of the authentic baptism of the Holy Spirit.

Our tradition and theirs both originated as revival movements that teach a work of divine grace in Christian life after conversion. Indeed, 20th-century Pentecostalism originated *in* the American Holiness Movement. The oldest Pentecostal denominations—including America's largest—are *both* Wesleyan-Holiness *and* Pentecostal in theology.

Sorting It Out

A distinction is sometimes made between Pentecostals and Charismatics, the latter also referred to as "neo-Pentecostals," though the distinction is less and less relevant. Pentecostalism emerged early in the 20th century. The Charismatic Movement sprang from a similar revival movement that began in the 1960s.

The Pentecostal/Charismatic landscape is divided into six major sectors:

- *Wesleyan-Holiness Pentecostals* emerged from the American Holiness Movement.
- *"Finished Work" Pentecostals* rejected entire sanctification and broke off from Wesleyan-Holiness Pentecostals.
- *"Jesus Only" or "Unitarian" Pentecostals* deny the doctrine of the Trinity and teach that Jesus is the name of God and that believers should be baptized only in Jesus' name; they broke off from the Finished Work people.
- *Charismatic fellowships* exist within most mainline denominations (including the Roman Catholic Church) or are nondenominational or interdenominational (like the Full Gospel Businessmen's Association).
- *New Charismatic denominations*, such as Calvary Chapel and the Vineyard Fellowship, are emerging from the Charismatic Movement of the 1960s and 1970s.
- The fringe of independent radical churches and ministries.

All six sectors embrace "the gifts of the Holy Spirit" mentioned by Paul: speaking in unknown tongues, interpretation of tongues, prophecy, and healing. Indeed, a significant difference between our classical Wesleyan-Holiness tradition and the Pentecostal/Charismatic traditions is this: the Wesleyan way of salvation and discipleship is wrapped up in the "fruit of the Spirit," while Pentecostals and Charismatics focus their worship and community around the "gifts of the Spirit."

The Apostolic Faith Movement

Charles F. Parham is considered the founder of modern Pentecostalism. He pastored a Methodist church in Eudora, Kansas, but did not pursue ordination, claiming a dislike for Methodist bishops and church order. He became a freelance evangelist, conducting revivals in eastern Kansas. He emphasized faith healing and Christ's premillennial second coming, and established a faith home and school of evangelism in Topeka.

In 1900 Parham asked the students to study Acts and identify any outward signs that could be interpreted as "the initial evidence" of the baptism of the Holy Spirit. The students concluded that speaking in tongues could qualify as that sign. Parham agreed and urged the students to seek it. On January 1, 1901, a woman spoke in tongues after a New Year's Eve watchnight service. Parham and others also did so in coming days.

Parham and his disciples believed that they were speaking in known but unlearned languages, not tongues of angels. They were confident this gift of languages would enable them to play an important role in world evangelization. The movement came to be called the Apostolic Faith. Its theology emphasized

- conversion,
- entire sanctification as a second work of grace,
- baptism of the Holy Spirit with tongues as the initial evidence.

The baptism of the Holy Spirit was separated from entire sanctification and defined as a separate and third work of grace, with tongues verifying its reception.

Azusa Street

A Black Holiness evangelist named William J. Seymour (1870—1922) was one of Parham's students a few years later in Houston. Parham was not inclined to challenge the mores of the segregated South, so Seymour listened to lectures from the hallway while white students sat in the classroom. Yet the segregated Seymour—the "least of these"—became a significant figure in Pentecostal history.

Seymour went to Los Angeles to preach in 1906. When his Apostolic Faith theology was rejected by the Holiness group that had brought him, he opened an independent mission on Azusa Street and started a revival meeting that has become one of the most famous ever. The secular and religious press gave it considerable attention. Evangelists and visitors from around the nation knelt at Seymour's altar and spoke in tongues, receiving the "baptism of the Holy Spirit." The meetings continued for over three years, and the Azusa Street revival's influence radiated to virtually every part of the United States and Canada, and even to Europe, Asia, and Africa. The mission evolved into a church that Seymour pastored until his death.

Principal Branches of Pentecostalism Today

Pentecostal Holiness Churches (Three Works of Grace)

Proselytes took the Apostolic Faith's theology to the South and Midwest, where the first Pentecostal denominations were formed. Three major denominations emerged that embraced the three-works-of-grace theology.

The Church of God in Christ. The Church of God in Christ today reports a membership of 5.5 million members. A predominantly African-American church, it originated in 1895 as a Wesleyan-Holiness denomination. The Church of God in Christ has grown rapidly in the past three decades. The largest Pentecostal denomination in America, it is also the largest church that teaches entire sanctification as a second work of grace. Local bishops govern the denomination.

Pentecostal Holiness Church. The Pentecostal Holiness Church was organized in the early 1900s. Its most significant early leader was Joseph H. King. Now named the International Pentecostal Holiness Church, its headquarters are in Bethany, Oklahoma, a short distance from Southern Nazarene University. Oral Roberts was raised in a Pentecostal Holiness parsonage and was its best-known preacher in the 1950s.[1] The church currently has just over 150,000 members in the United States.[2]

The Church of God (Cleveland, Tennessee). The Christian Union, founded in 1886, became the nucleus of a small connection of Holiness churches in Tennessee. Tongues-speaking was a characteristic by 1896. Today the Church of God (Cleveland, Tennessee) has over 722,500 members in the United States, nearly 8,000 in Canada, and almost 4 million worldwide. The church does not ordain women but permits them to preach and serve as evangelists. It observes the ordinances of baptism by immersion, the Lord's Supper, and foot washing.[3]

The Finished Work Controversy

Pentecostalism grew theologically diverse as it proliferated. William H. Durham (1873—1912), a former Baptist, was one of the first to publicly challenge the underlying Holiness teachings in early Pentecostalism. Durham's North Avenue Mission in Chicago was an important link in spreading Pentecostalism to Brazil, Italy, and South America. By 1910 Durham was preaching against entire sanctification. Historian William Menzies states that Durham was convinced that the doctrine was vague and could not be verified in a tangible way.

Instead, Durham articulated a view known in Pentecostal circles as "the finished work of Calvary" theory of sanctification. He taught that the problem of sin in the Christian life is dealt with at conversion and that the unfolding of this work in the Christian life is a gradual process of sanctification.[4]

Durham's arguments persuaded former Baptists like himself and others with a background of mild Calvinism. Through his advocacy, a second round of denominations emerged. Those uncomfortable with the doctrine of entire sanctification withdrew from the earlier Pentecostal churches and formed church bodies more compatible with their beliefs.

The Assemblies of God. The most prominent denomination to spring from the Finished Work controversy was the Assemblies of God, organized in 1914 at Hot Springs, Arkansas. It spread rapidly in the South and in major cities across the United States. By the 1950s it was penetrating smaller Midwestern towns, and by 1995 it reported just under 1.4 million full members and an inclusive membership of 2.3 million for the United States. Its worldwide membership is much higher: over 22 million members.[5]

International Church of the Foursquare Gospel. Aimee Semple McPherson, a flamboyant evangelist, was a former Salvation Army worker. She was ordained by William Durham and developed a popular evangelistic career as "Sister Aimee." In 1923 she dedicated the 5,300-seat Angelus Temple in Los Angeles, the "mother church" of what developed into the International Church of the Foursquare Gospel. The church's four primary theological principles emphasize Jesus as Savior, Baptizer (with the Holy Spirit), Healer, and Coming King. Today the International Church of the Foursquare Gospel has just over 2 million members worldwide, of which over 224,000 live in the United States.[6]

Oneness Pentecostalism

The Assemblies of God church was only months old when a controversy shattered its peace. Evangelist Frank Ewart began preaching that baptism was to be administered in the name of Jesus only, not in the name of "the Father, Son, and Holy Spirit." This was based on several places in Acts in which groups were said to "believe in the name of Jesus" and were baptized in His name. Ewart and other supporters were forced to defend their interpretation in light of Jesus' own words: "Go into all the world . . . baptizing . . . in the name of the Father and of the Son and of the Holy Spirit" (Mark 16:15; Matt. 28:19).

As the "Jesus only" folk marshaled evidence for their baptismal formula, their basic concept of God shifted until they denied the doctrine of the Trinity altogether. Oneness Pentecostals came to hold that Trinitarianism is really tritheism—belief in three Gods, not one. They asserted that "Jesus" is the true name of the one God and that "Father, Son, and Holy Spirit" are merely *titles*. Thus, when Jesus says to baptize "in the name of the Father and of the Son and of the Holy Spirit," the reference is to the *name* (Jesus), which these *titles* signify.

Oneness Pentecostals, then and now, hold that those who have not been baptized by the correct formula are not true Christians, since they have not fulfilled Jesus' command. The two major oneness Pentecostal bodies today are the Pentecostal Assemblies of the World and The United Pentecostal Church International.

The Charismatic Movement

Different strands of Pentecostalism influenced the Charismatic Movement that developed in the 1960s. It began (by most reckonings) with Episcopal priest Dennis Bennett's acceptance of the Pentecostal experience in 1959. Instead of joining a Pentecostal denomination, Bennett remained at St. Mark's Episcopal Church in Van Nuys, California, and led a Pentecostal revival there. Eventually, opponents of that emphasis forced him out, but Bennett simply took his Pentecostal ministry to another Episcopal parish. The pattern was repeated by clergy in Lutheran, Methodist, Presbyterian, and Roman Catholic churches, among others. The neo-Pentecostal revival was on.

Neo-Pentecostal magazines appeared, like *New Wine Magazine* and *Charisma*. Bible studies and prayer groups formed, bringing together folks from many different denominations. Charismatics and old-line Pentecostals took roles in the Jesus People Movement of the 1960s and 1970s as Evangelicals reached out to the alienated youth culture. Charismatic campus ministries also developed.

Many people were surprised by the Charismatic Movement's strength within the Roman Catholic Church. Catholic colleges and universities became centers of a new Pentecostalism faithful to church dogma but free in worship style and firm in its belief in the baptism in the

Holy Spirit and the restoration of Charismatic gifts to the Church. Even some Catholic theologians were active in the Charismatic revival.

By the early 1990s, an estimated 50 to 65 million Catholics worldwide had been touched at some point in their life by the Charismatic renewal movement. This included an estimated 10 million American Catholics. About one-half million American Catholics were still active in 1992, gathered largely into some 5,000 prayer and Bible study cells.

New Charismatic Denominations

The Charismatic revival has spawned new denominational groups, just as the early-20th-century Pentecostal revival did.

Calvary Chapel. Calvary Chapel began in 1965 through the ministry of Chuck Smith, former Foursquare Gospel preacher, whose effective outreach to hippies propelled him to a leadership position in the Jesus Movement on the West Coast. Calvary Chapel has strongly influenced contemporary Christian music through its Maranatha! Music company. Larry Taylor, a teacher within the church, states that Calvary Chapel takes the middle ground between Fundamentalism and Pentecostalism, emphasizing the gifts of the Spirit but moderating their use by adhering to scriptural restrictions on their use. By 1997 there were about 700 congregations worldwide, nearly 600 of them in North America.

Vineyard Christian Fellowship. The Vineyard began in 1973 through the ministry of Kenn Gullikson, a Jesus Movement pastor. In the early 1980s, John Wimber led a large congregation once affiliated with Calvary Chapel into the Vineyard fellowship. With Gullikson's blessing, he became the movement's primary leader. The Vineyard emphasizes "signs and wonders"—miraculous elements that include divine healings, exorcisms, and prophecy. In 1991 there were about 330 churches, mostly in North America.[7]

Charismatic Episcopal Church. The Charismatic Episcopal Church represents a growing phenomenon: churches seeking to recover a broad catholic tradition while remaining attuned to the Holy Spirit. This denomination was founded at a conference of independent churches held in Kansas City in 1992 and had about 200 congregations by 1997. It is episcopally governed, and churches typically follow the Episcopal Church's 1928 or 1979 editions of the *Book of Common Prayer,* but they are free to adopt another ancient rite of worship if they choose. At the same time, the Charismatic Episcopal Church emphasizes divine healing and spiritual gifts.[8]

The Fanatical Fringe

The solid, middle-of-the-road Christians in Pentecostal and Charismatic denominations and churches have been embarrassed by the fanatical fringe of the movement. Scores of independent churches, clusters of churches, small denominations, television evangelists, and certain specialized ministries have heaped shame on the movement. Most are led by powerful persons with giant egos. They head up ministries that often make their leaders wealthy.

The Shepherding Movement, launched in the 1960s from Florida and Alabama by Bob Mumford and three associates, appears to have deeply damaged many sincere believers. The Shepherding Movement grew quickly to about 100,000 adherents. Its *New Wine Magazine* had a circulation of 90,000 (larger than *Christianity Today* at the time). It was shipped to 120 countries. Up to a half-million audiotapes were marketed annually during the 1970s and 1980s. Its dramatic evangelistic and church growth methods were soon aped by other Charismatic groups such as Crossroads, Maranatha Christian Churches, the Set Free Christian Fellowship, and others. That the Shepherding Movement made slaves and robots of its disciples—especially women—was seldom noticed at first.

But Shepherding Movement victims began to fill the counselors' schedules all over the country. Deeply troubled, unable to trust anyone, void of self-esteem, and deeply wounded, these people, according to David Seamands, "needed help sorting the true from the false. . . . I have seen serious psychological damage caused by these movements. . . . The repressive relationships and . . . giving up personal autonomy to a pastor/leader can result in a loss of identity."[9]

Respected Pentecostal pastor Jack Hayford states that "multiplied thousands of pastors, like myself, have spent large amounts of time over the last 15 years picking up the pieces of broken lives that resulted from distortion of truth by extreme teachings and destructive applications on discipleship, authority, and shepherding."[10]

What Pentecostals Want You to Know

In 1981 the late Thomas F. Zimmerman, then the highest official in the Assemblies of God, addressed other Christians on the topic of Pentecostalism's priorities and beliefs. At the time, it was estimated that there were over 50 million Pentecostals worldwide. But Pentecostals, Zimmerman said, cannot be judged successful because they are numerous; groups teaching heresy have also grown numerous. Rather, Pentecostals can be judged successful because they, by and large, have remained faithful to these characteristics:

- They hold a high view of Scripture.
- They affirm the great central convictions of the Christian tradition.
- They "honor the Father, Son, and Holy Spirit equally."
- They take seriously the Great Commission.
- They seek to be responsive to the Holy Spirit.
- They cooperate with other Evangelicals and helped to found the National Association of Evangelicals.

Some people "believe that the main message of Pentecostalism is the baptism of the Holy Spirit and speaking in tongues," but that is not the case, according to Zimmerman. Pentecostalism's principal message is that the gospel of Jesus Christ can save us from our sins, he said. Zimmerman noted that "almost all Pentecostals today believe that a person who has accepted Christ is indwelt by the Spirit. . . . Pentecostals differentiate between the Holy Spirit baptizing believers into the body of Christ (1 Cor. 12:13) and Christ baptizing them in the Holy Spirit (Matt. 3:11-12; Acts 1:5)."[11]

The American Holiness Movement and the early Pentecostal Movement sprang from the same social milieu. But they have gone different directions in important matters. Along with other denominations that have watched the Pentecostal/Charismatic Movement develop, the Church of the Nazarene has resisted many of its claims. To those concerns we turn in the next chapter.

AT A GLANCE

NAZARENES IN DIALOGUE WITH THE PENTECOSTALS AND CHARISMATICS

Historical Background

Nazarenes and the Pentecostals have had a tense dialogue since the early days of both movements. Early Nazarenes felt that the emotionalism, tongues-speaking, and doctrine of the Pentecostals were destructive to the Nazarene vision and mission.

The birth of the Charismatic Movement in the 1960s did little to ease tensions. In recent years, however, serious efforts at dialogue—though not close union—have been made.

Core Beliefs of Pentecostals and Charismatics

The extreme diversity of the Pentecostal and Charismatic Movements makes generalizing hazardous, but most of these groups adhere to the following beliefs:

1. The authority of Scripture
2. Salvation by grace through faith
3. Born-again conversion
4. The baptism with the Holy Spirit
5. Entire sanctification (embraced by some)
6. Three works of grace
7. Speaking in tongues as evidence of baptism with the Spirit and as a prayer language
8. Denial of the Trinity by some
9. Theology of prosperity (preached by many Pentecostals/Charismatics)

Agreement and Differences

Nazarenes share common ground on the first four core beliefs listed above but strenuously reject beliefs 6, 7, 8, and 9. They also question the preparation of clergy and the lack of the discipline of clergy as practiced in some wings of the Pentecostal/Charismatic Movement.

Wesleyan-Holiness and Pentecostal/Charismatic Dialogue Today

Pastors report that many former Pentecostals/Charismatics are joining Nazarene churches. In many cases these believers are willing to give up or refrain from teaching the practice of tongues-speaking.

In 1998 the Wesleyan Theological Society and the Association for Pentecostal Studies held a joint meeting. Scholars from both sides explored the commonalities and differences of the two traditions. It is too early to tell to what extent this meeting will determine how well these parties can walk and work together.

It is strangely and profoundly in touch with the postmodern age, which seeks suprarational or subrational escape from reason, science, and technology.

CHAPTER 15

NAZARENES IN DIALOGUE WITH THE PENTECOSTALS AND CHARISMATICS

ONE THING IS CERTAIN—Evangelicals can learn a lot from the Pentecostal/Charismatic (P/C) Movement. They wrote the book on church growth—metaphorically and literally. About 60 percent of all Christian books sold are bought by Pentecostals and Charismatics. They can also coach other churches on fervent evangelism. And does any group make religion more direct and personal than the P/Cs? They have connected with the man and woman on the street in making religious experience relevant to felt needs.

Our P/C brothers and sisters in Christ have often modeled exemplary consecration. They have taught everyone how to make worship warmhearted and celebrative. They have carried the banner in seeking to let the Holy Spirit lead in worship and in life.

Yet for all this, a number of things in P/C theology and practice are troublesome. Nazarenes, with believers in other denominations, have watched the P/C Movement emerge and grow and have rejected many of its claims.

Early Nazarene Evaluations

The first generation of Nazarenes witnessed Pentecostalism's rise. R. L. Averill, a Southern revivalist, published an early account of the Apostolic Faith Movement in the Houston area, which he began observing in 1906: "We have a new movement in our midst. . . . Doctrinally they have as yet no well defined statement for while some say we must be converted and sanctified and afterwards receive the baptism of the Holy Ghost which is always evidenced by speaking with other tongues; yet others are claiming that a sinner may at one and the same time get pardoned, sanctified wholly and baptised [with the Spirit] and speak with tongues. I saw this at Oxford. . . . Truly we are in a fast age."

Averill noted "good consecrated, conscientious people among them" but concluded that others "are not so," adding: "I don't know a more divided discordant people. There seemed to be only one point of agreement among them and that is every one should speak in tongues." His verdict: "The work does not bear the stamp of deep spirituality to my mind."[1]

Although common soil and kinship surrounded the Holiness and Pentecostal movements, sharply divergent views about the nature of the Holy Spirit's work separated the two traditions. The early Nazarenes rejected the Pentecostal-Holiness message because it

- taught that the baptism of the Holy Spirit was completely separate from entire sanctification and was a third work of grace;
- focused on the gifts of the Spirit rather than the fruit of the Spirit, around which entire sanctification is chiefly oriented;
- emphasized speaking in tongues as the "initial evidence" of Holy Spirit baptism.

Thoroughly Wesleyan, the early Nazarenes believed in the inner and outer witness of God's Spirit to conversion and to entire sanctification. The inner witness: a quiet but sure confidence in God's grace. The outer witness: not tongues or any other phenomena, but the actual life of holiness as a certain witness to others.

There was one other reason for the Nazarene rejection of Pentecostalism: early Nazarenes were unafraid of emotion in religion, but they regarded the distinctive forms of Pentecostal religion as errant and humanistic emotionalism. They often referred to Pentecostal tongues-speaking, prophecies, and "interpretation of tongues" as "delusions."

Contemporary Dialogue

There can be no doubt that the Holiness Movement (including the Nazarenes) and the P/C Movement have not always treated each other as brothers and sisters in Christ. Sometimes the interchanges—like a family feud—were harsh and vindictive. We are doing better these days, but the two movements, like brothers who have gone their separate ways, are far apart on some issues.

Doctrinal Differences

At least eight doctrinal differences loom between Nazarenes and the P/C Movement.

1. The Trinity. "Jesus Only" or "Oneness" Pentecostals deny the Holy Trinity. Nothing could be more heterodox as far as orthodox Christians, including Nazarenes, are concerned.

2. Baptism. Our primary problem here is with Oneness Pentecostals who teach that converts are to be baptized in the name of "Jesus only." Those who are baptized in the name of the Father, Son, and Holy Spirit (the standard Christian formula for 2,000 years) are not Christians at all, according to Oneness Pentecostals.

3. Three Works of Grace. Even the Pentecostals who agree with the Nazarenes on entire sanctification as a second definite work of grace add a third work—baptism with the Holy Spirit. We teach that the baptism with the Spirit is part and parcel of entire sanctification and not a third work.

4. Entire Sanctification. We teach that entire sanctification comes after conversion and that in this experience the heart is cleansed from all sin. Many P/C churches teach a second work of grace in which the Christian is empowered by the Spirit for service but deny that inbred sin is cleansed.

5. Speaking in Tongues. A consistent thread in Nazarene teaching on the gifts of the Spirit is that speaking in tongues, as recorded in Acts and elsewhere in the New Testament, was the supernatural gift of speaking known languages. This is evident in the Pentecost narrative (Acts 2) and again in subsequent passages in Acts in which "speaking in tongues" is referenced. The earliest Pentecostals held this view as well until they discovered that they were unable to communicate with those of other languages through their "gift of tongues."

The instances in Acts in which speaking in tongues occurs are associated with the giving of the Holy Spirit to a new group of people: to Jewish followers of Jesus (chap. 2), to the household of the Roman soldier Cornelius (chap. 10), and to the Ephesians (chap. 19). In the most fundamental sense, the giving of the gift of languages at Pentecost signaled powerfully the Holy Spirit's acceptance of all nations and races in the new Christian Church. Subsequent instances in Acts in which languages were given drive home this point: they re-create the first Pentecost among different groups of people previously separated from Jewish Christians by the law.

Nazarenes teach that "the gift of tongues is related to the miraculous gift of many languages on the Day of Pentecost. On that great day the Church was enabled to cross language barriers. The people present were astonished because each one heard the gospel being preached in his own native dialect (Acts 2:6, 8). This special miracle was an expression of God's desire to reach every man everywhere through the spoken and written word. Language is the vehicle of God's truth."[2]

Only in Corinthians is "tongues" mentioned as a feature in worship. The Charismatic Movement, picking up on this, made speaking in tongues a personal prayer language.

But did Paul mean to promote tongues as a spiritual gift, or did he try to restrict it? Christians can disagree reasonably with one another over how to interpret Paul, but Nazarene teaching on this matter has been clear: Paul says that although he speaks in tongues more than any of the Corinthians, he would rather speak 5 words in a known language than 10,000 words in a language unintelligible to hearers (1 Cor. 14:18-19). And why? Because clarity promotes the gospel of Jesus Christ, while confusion hinders its spread.

It is difficult to know, let alone prove, exactly what the gift of tongues in New Testament times really was. It was divinely bestowed. Was it a grace that enabled people to witness across language barriers? Was it gibberish like what the Greek mystery cults practiced? Was it a supernatural gift of a divine language understood only by superhuman entities or spirits?

No one can prove what it was. Its practice, essence, and significance are shrouded in mystery. Since tongues-speaking is so hard to pin down, it seems prudent not to make it the cornerstone or even a major plank in one's theological platform. Nazarenes patently reject the P/C insistence that tongues-speaking is the evidence of the baptism with the Holy Spirit. The *Manual* states,

> The Church of the Nazarene believes that the Holy Spirit bears witness to the new birth and to the subsequent work of heart cleansing, or entire sanctification, through the infilling of the Holy Spirit.
>
> We affirm that the one biblical evidence of entire sanctification, or the infilling of the Holy Spirit, is the cleansing of the heart by faith from original sin as stated in Acts 15:8-9: "God, who knows the heart, showed them that he accepted them by giving the Holy Spirit to them, just as he did to us. He made no distinction between us and them, for he purified their hearts by faith." And this cleansing is manifested by the fruit of the Spirit in a holy life. . . .
>
> To affirm that even a special or any alleged physical evidence, or "prayer language," is evidence of the baptism with the Spirit is contrary to the biblical and historic position of the church.[3]

6. Doctrine of the Holy Spirit. The Church of the Nazarene witnessed Pentecostalism's emergence and, with other classically Wesleyan churches, rejected many of its claims about the nature of the Spirit's role in salvation. What, then, do we teach about the Holy Spirit? A good summary is found in H. Ray Dunning's *Grace, Faith, and Holiness.* We believe that

- to each person the Holy Spirit restores a measure of the free will lost through original sin.
- the Holy Spirit prepares each of us for salvation by awakening us to an awareness of our sin before God.
- the Holy Spirit is the Creator and Dispenser of faith, who gives justifying faith at the moment of conversion and throughout the Christian walk.
- the Holy Spirit renews us inwardly at conversion through the new birth, or regeneration, by planting a new spiritual life within.
- the Holy Spirit assures us that our sins are forgiven and that we are God's children.
- the Holy Spirit is the active Agent in progressive sanctification, or growth in holiness, as God renews us continually in His own image.
- the Holy Spirit is the active Agent in the entire sanctification of believers as our hearts are filled with divine love.
- the Holy Spirit in us is the basis of our hope of resurrection (Rom. 8:11).[4]

Dunning notes two errors about the Holy Spirit that Christian groups often make. One is to retreat into legalism and freeze out the Holy Spirit. Paul opposed that error among the churches of Galatia. The other error is to fall into libertinism—to carry freedom in the Spirit to an extreme. This was the error Paul opposed in the Corinthian church. He listed the spiritual gifts that the Corinthians claimed to enjoy—speaking and interpretation of tongues, prophecy, and spiritual discernment—and still said that they had missed the main point: the divine love in one's heart and life, which is the most important and enduring of the Spirit's gifts.

7. Signs and Wonders and Healing Miracles. Some Pentecostal and Charismatic groups promote signs and wonders. This leads to sensationalism, pseudomiracles, and in the end, disillusionment of believers. Overemphasis on healing often leads to excluding proper medical care. Some groups declare that God is obligated to heal every sick person if the victim's faith is genuine. One Indiana sect reportedly has been responsible for "one preventable death per month" for 15 years by forbidding members to seek medical treatment.[5] Prayer is all they need, they say. This is an independent church led by a renegade preacher, and his abuse cannot be charged to any denomination.

The Nazarene article of faith on divine healing came about during the "healing revival," and it lets everyone know that Nazarenes are to seek medical treatment as well as use prayer in times of illness.

8. Theology of Prosperity. Some P/C groups and preachers, especially televangelists, preach that financial prosperity lies ahead for all God's children—especially if they'll put a check in the mail to them today! We believe that following God with all one's heart does not necessarily make him or her wealthy. Also, a substantial bank account is no testimony at all to God's blessing or to the advanced spiritual standing of the person whose name is on the account ledger. How wealthy was Jesus, Paul, Brother Lawrence, or Mother Teresa?

Differences of Practice and Philosophy

Every faith tradition has vulnerabilities. Nazarenes, as we saw in chapter 1, know that they need to guard against legalism and the loss of proper confession of sin. A number of predictable vulnerabilities mark the P/C movement as well.

1. Anti-intellectualism. "The only thing worse than an old [experienced] Christian is an educated one," declared Charismatic pastor Phil Aguilar of the Set Free Christian Fellowship.[6] A young disciple with an intellectual bent who attended Wayland Mitchell's La Puerta or Christian Fellowship Church was called an "educated idiot with a high IQ" by his pastor.[7]

Nazarenes have their own problems with anti-intellectualism. As the young denomination was forming, the world as they knew it was shattered by German biblical criticism, Darwin's evolutionary theory, Dewey's philosophical pragmatism ("Truth is what works"), and theological modernism. As Nazarene pioneers surveyed this battlefield, they noticed that the ones who had destroyed what they had always believed about the origin, nature, and destiny of the Bible, Christianity, and the human race were folks who could read Greek and Latin, people with university degrees. Part of their reaction was a predictable anti-intellectualism. They distrusted education not done under the supervision of the church. The tendency to anti-intellectualism is a vulnerability that we share with our P/C friends.

2. Religious Experience at the Expense of Careful Thought. The strong emphasis on religious experience among P/C groups can result in a definite lack of critical thinking. "You get the experience, and the doctrine won't bother you." Some say Nazarenes, too, have coped with this vulnerability but seem to have made more progress toward balancing critical thought and religious experience than some P/C groups. When ecstatic experience, high emotion, and speaking in tongues is the principal focus of religion, critical thinking just weighs less.

3. Preparation and Discipline of Clergy. The anti-intellectual climate appears to have resulted in inadequate ministerial education. Enroth's study of abusive churches in the Charismatic Movement showed that their pastors had very little formal education for ministry. In many such churches, "the only theological education permitted for those called to ministry is to be done by the head pastor or his inner circle of 'clones.'"[8]

Christianity Today noted that the Charismatic revival in South America has produced 175,000 pastors without one day of ministerial education.[9] This could produce serious problems a decade hence. We are quite sure that the 21st century will require better-educated pastors, not barely educated pastors. For some reason, the P/C Movement has produced a bumper crop of bully pastors who are answerable to no one. "It's my way or the highway," one pastor announced.[10] "God wants you to do what I ask you to do. . . . If you don't, you're going against God himself," declared another.

No one can discipline these bully preachers, it seems. And while their antics cannot be charged to the good rank-and-file members of P/C churches, observers raise the question: Is there something in the movement's message or method that makes such abuse possible by the misguided, the manipulative, or the unscrupulous? Enroth apparently thinks so. For example, while he does not charge the Vineyard Fellowship with abuse, he notes that its structures, procedures, and emphasis on power and signs and wonders make it vulnerable to manipulative abuse. Among those who seem to go discipline-free are several P/C televangelists whose sexual and financial transgressions and multiple marriages and divorces scandalize the gospel and the Church.

4. Divisiveness. The P/C Movement has been extraordinarily fractious among themselves. But the divisiveness they often bring to other fellowships is unsettling to some. When a cluster of Charismatics move into a non-Charismatic church, there is more than a little fear and trembling about church unity. Often those with the gift of tongues feel so strongly about it that they cannot keep from sharing it with everyone else in the church. Nazarenes have not generally felt it their duty to infiltrate the Pentecostal ranks and change their doctrine. But the reverse has not always been the case. Even at the 1997 General Assembly in San Antonio, pro-tongues persons tried hard to "evangelize" the 1,100 delegates on the point of "baptizing" several kinds of tongues-speaking.[11]

There is evidence that this problem is lessening. Some Nazarene pastors report that many former P/C church members have come to the Church of the Nazarene. Many still believe in tongues or practice a "prayer language," but they prudently refrain from making an issue of these matters and faithfully support the pastor and the church.

In exploring the areas in which we disagree with our P/C friends, to quote the Board of General Superintendents, "we do not wish to reflect on the sincerity or integrity of those who differ with us on these matters. We recognize as fellow members of His universal body all who are in Christ and extend to them the right hand of Christian fellowship."[12]

APPENDIX

ARTICLES OF FAITH

I. The Triune God

1. We believe in one eternally existent, infinite God, Sovereign of the universe; that He only is God, creative and administrative, holy in nature, attributes, and purpose; that He, as God, is Triune in essential being, revealed as Father, Son, and Holy Spirit.

II. Jesus Christ

2. We believe in Jesus Christ, the Second Person of the Triune Godhead; that He was eternally one with the Father; that He became incarnate by the Holy Spirit and was born of the Virgin Mary, so that two whole and perfect natures, that is to say the Godhead and manhood, are thus united in one Person very God and very man, the God-man.

We believe that Jesus Christ died for our sins, and that He truly arose from the dead and took again His body, together with all things appertaining to the perfection of man's nature, wherewith He ascended into heaven and is there engaged in intercession for us.

III. The Holy Spirit

3. We believe in the Holy Spirit, the Third Person of the Triune Godhead, that He is ever present and efficiently active in and with the Church of Christ, convincing the world of sin, regenerating those who repent and believe, sanctifying believers, and guiding into all truth as it is in Jesus.

IV. The Holy Scriptures

4. We believe in the plenary inspiration of the Holy Scriptures, by which we understand the 66 books of the Old and New Testaments, given by divine inspiration, inerrantly revealing the will of God concerning us in all things necessary to our salvation, so that whatever is not contained therein is not to be enjoined as an article of faith.

V. Sin, Original and Personal

5. We believe that sin came into the world through the disobedience of our first parents, and death by sin. We believe that sin is of two kinds: original sin or depravity, and actual or personal sin.

5.1. We believe that original sin, or depravity, is that corruption of the nature of all the offspring of Adam by reason of which everyone is very far gone from original righteousness or the pure state of our first parents at the time of their creation, is averse to God, is without spiritual life, and inclined to evil, and that continually. We further believe that original sin continues to exist with the new life of the regenerate, until eradicated by the baptism with the Holy Spirit.

5.2. We believe that original sin differs from actual sin in that it constitutes an inherited propensity to actual sin for which no one is accountable until its divinely provided remedy is neglected or rejected.

5.3. We believe that actual or personal sin is a voluntary violation of a known law of God by a morally responsible person. It is therefore not to be confused with involuntary and inescapable shortcomings, infirmities, faults, mistakes, failures, or other deviations from a standard of perfect conduct that are the residual effects of the Fall. However, such innocent effects do not include attitudes or responses contrary to the spirit of Christ, which may properly be called sins of the spirit. We believe that personal sin is primarily and essentially a violation of the law of love; and that in relation to Christ sin may be defined as unbelief.

VI. Atonement

6. We believe that Jesus Christ, by His sufferings, by the shedding of His own blood, and by His meritorious death on the Cross, made a full atonement for all human sin, and that this Atonement is the only ground of salvation, and that it is sufficient for every individual of Adam's race. The Atonement is graciously efficacious for the salvation of the irresponsible

and for the children in innocency but is efficacious for the salvation of those who reach the age of responsibility only when they repent and believe.

VII. Free Agency

7. We believe that the human race's creation in Godlikeness included ability to choose between right and wrong, and that thus human beings were made morally responsible; that through the fall of Adam they became depraved so that they cannot now turn and prepare themselves by their own natural strength and works to faith and calling upon God. But we also believe that the grace of God through Jesus Christ is freely bestowed upon all people, enabling all who will to turn from sin to righteousness, believe on Jesus Christ for pardon and cleansing from sin, and follow good works pleasing and acceptable in His sight.

We believe that all persons, though in the possession of the experience of regeneration and entire sanctification, may fall from grace and apostatize and, unless they repent of their sins, be hopelessly and eternally lost.

VIII. Repentance

8. We believe that repentance, which is a sincere and thorough change of the mind in regard to sin, involving a sense of personal guilt and a voluntary turning away from sin, is demanded of all who have by act or purpose become sinners against God. The Spirit of God gives to all who will repent the gracious help of penitence of heart and hope of mercy, that they may believe unto pardon and spiritual life.

IX. Justification, Regeneration, and Adoption

9. We believe that justification is the gracious and judicial act of God by which He grants full pardon of all guilt and complete release from the penalty of sins committed, and acceptance as righteous, to all who believe on Jesus Christ and receive Him as Lord and Savior.

10. We believe that regeneration, or the new birth, is that gracious work of God whereby the moral nature of the repentant believer is spiritually quickened and given a distinctively spiritual life, capable of faith, love, and obedience.

11. We believe that adoption is that gracious act of God by which the justified and regenerated believer is constituted a son of God.

12. We believe that justification, regeneration, and adoption are simultaneous in the experience of seekers after God and are obtained upon the condition of faith, preceded by repentance; and that to this work and state of grace the Holy Spirit bears witness.

X. Entire Sanctification

13. We believe that entire sanctification is that act of God, subsequent to regeneration, by which believers are made free from original sin, or depravity, and brought into a state of entire devotement to God, and the holy obedience of love made perfect.

It is wrought by the baptism with the Holy Spirit, and comprehends in one experience the cleansing of the heart from sin and the abiding, indwelling presence of the Holy Spirit, empowering the believer for life and service.

Entire sanctification is provided by the blood of Jesus, is wrought instantaneously by faith, preceded by entire consecration; and to this work and state of grace the Holy Spirit bears witness.

This experience is also known by various terms representing its different phases, such as "Christian perfection," "perfect love," "heart purity," "the baptism with the Holy Spirit," "the fullness of the blessing," and "Christian holiness."

14. We believe that there is a marked distinction between a pure heart and a mature character. The former is obtained in an instant, the result of entire sanctification; the latter is the result of growth in grace.

We believe that the grace of entire sanctification includes the impulse to grow in grace. However, this impulse must be consciously nurtured, and careful attention given to the requisites and processes of spiritual development and improvement in Christlikeness of character and personality. Without such purposeful endeavor one's witness may be impaired and the grace itself frustrated and ultimately lost.

XI. The Church

15. We believe in the Church, the community that confesses Jesus Christ as Lord, the covenant people of God made new in Christ, the Body of Christ called together by the Holy Spirit through the Word.

God calls the Church to express its life in the unity and fellowship of the Spirit; in worship through the preaching of the Word, observance of the sacraments, and ministry in His name; by obedience to Christ and mutual accountability.

The mission of the Church in the world is to continue the redemptive work of Christ in the power of the Spirit through holy living, evangelism, discipleship, and service.

The Church is a historical reality, which organizes itself in culturally conditioned forms; exists both as local congregations and as a universal body; sets apart persons called of God for specific ministries. God calls the Church to live under His rule in anticipation of the consummation at the coming of our Lord Jesus Christ.

XII. Baptism

16. We believe that Christian baptism, commanded by our Lord, is a sacrament signifying acceptance of the benefits of the atonement of Jesus Christ, to be administered to believers and declarative of their faith in Jesus Christ as their Savior, and full purpose of obedience in holiness and righteousness.

Baptism being a symbol of the new covenant, young children may be baptized, upon request of parents or guardians who shall give assurance for them of necessary Christian training.

Baptism may be administered by sprinkling, pouring, or immersion, according to the choice of the applicant.

XIII. The Lord's Supper

17. We believe that the Memorial and Communion Supper instituted by our Lord and Savior Jesus Christ is essentially a New Testament sacrament, declarative of His sacrificial death, through the merits of which believers have life and salvation and promise of all spiritual blessings in Christ. It is distinctively for those who are prepared for reverent appreciation of its significance, and by it they show forth the Lord's death till He come again. It being the Communion feast, only those who have faith in Christ and love for the saints should be called to participate therein.

XIV. Divine Healing[2]

18. We believe in the Bible doctrine of divine healing and urge our people to seek to offer the prayer of faith for the healing of the sick. [Providential means and agencies when deemed necessary should not be refused.] *We also believe God heals through the means of medical science.*

XV. Second Coming of Christ

19. We believe that the Lord Jesus Christ will come again; that we who are alive at His coming shall not precede them that are asleep in Christ Jesus; but that, if we are abiding in Him, we shall be caught up with the risen saints to meet the Lord in the air, so that we shall ever be with the Lord.

XVI. Resurrection, Judgment, and Destiny

20. We believe in the resurrection of the dead, that the bodies both of the just and of the unjust shall be raised to life and united with their spirits—"they that have done good, unto the resurrection of life; and they that have done evil, unto the resurrection of damnation."

21. We believe in future judgment in which every person shall appear before God to be judged according to his or her deeds in this life.

22. We believe that glorious and everlasting life is assured to all who savingly believe in, and obediently follow, Jesus Christ our Lord; and that the finally impenitent shall suffer eternally in hell.

---

2. Constitutional changes adopted by the 1997 General Assembly are in the process of ratification by the district assemblies at the time of printing. Where changes are being made, words in italics are new words and words in brackets [ ] are words being deleted.

THE CHURCH

I. The General Church

23. The Church of God is composed of all spiritually regenerate persons, whose names are written in heaven.

II. The Churches Severally

24. The churches severally are to be composed of such regenerate persons as by providential permission, and by the leadings of the Holy Spirit, become associated together for holy fellowship and ministries.

III. The Church of the Nazarene

25. The Church of the Nazarene is composed of those persons who have voluntarily associated themselves together according to the doctrines and polity of said church, and who seek holy Christian fellowship, the conversion of sinners, the entire sanctification of believers, their upbuilding in holiness, and the simplicity and spiritual power manifest in the primitive New Testament Church, together with the preaching of the gospel to every creature.

IV. Agreed Statement of Belief

26. Recognizing that the right and privilege of persons to church membership rest upon the fact of their being regenerate, we would require only such avowals of belief as are essential to Christian experience. We, therefore, deem belief in the following brief statements to be sufficient. We believe:

26.1. In one God—the Father, Son, and Holy Spirit.

26.2. That the Old and New Testament Scriptures, given by plenary inspiration, contain all truth necessary to faith and Christian living.

26.3. That man is born with a fallen nature, and is, therefore, inclined to evil, and that continually.

26.4. That the finally impenitent are hopelessly and eternally lost.

26.5. That the atonement through Jesus Christ is for the whole human race; and that whosoever repents and believes on the Lord Jesus Christ is justified and regenerated and saved from the dominion of sin.

26.6. That believers are to be sanctified wholly, subsequent to regeneration, through faith in the Lord Jesus Christ.

26.7. That the Holy Spirit bears witness to the new birth, and also to the entire sanctification of believers.

26.8. That our Lord will return, the dead will be raised, and the final judgment will take place.

V. The General Rules

27. To be identified with the visible Church is the blessed privilege and sacred duty of all who are saved from their sins and are seeking completeness in Christ Jesus. It is required of all who desire to unite with the Church of the Nazarene, and thus to walk in fellowship with us, that they shall show evidence of salvation from their sins by a godly walk and vital piety; and that they shall be, or earnestly desire to be, cleansed from all indwelling sin. They shall evidence their commitment to God—

27.1. FIRST. By doing that which is enjoined in the Word of God, which is our rule of both faith and practice, including:

(1) Loving God with all the heart, soul, mind, and strength, and one's neighbor as oneself (Exodus 20:3-6; Leviticus 19:17-18; Deuteronomy 5:7-10; 6:4-5; Mark 12:28-31; Romans 13:8-10).

(2) Pressing upon the attention of the unsaved the claims of the gospel, inviting them to the house of the Lord, and trying to compass their salvation (Matthew 28:19-20; Acts 1:8; Romans 1:14-16; 2 Corinthians 5:18-20).

(3) Being courteous to all men (Ephesians 4:32; Titus 3:2; 1 Peter 2:17; 1 John 3:18).

(4) Being helpful to those who are also of the faith, in love forbearing one another (Romans 12:13; Galatians 6:2, 10; Colossians 3:12-14).

(5) Seeking to do good to the bodies and souls of men; feeding the hungry, clothing the naked, visiting the sick and imprisoned, and ministering to the needy, as opportunity and ability are given (Matthew 25:35-36; 2 Corinthians 9:8-10; Galatians 2:10; James 2:15-16; 1 John 3:17-18).

(6) Contributing to the support of the ministry and the church and its work in tithes and offerings (Malachi 3:10; Luke 6:38; 1 Corinthians 9:14; 16:2; 2 Corinthians 9:6-10; Philippians 4:15-19).

(7) Attending faithfully all the ordinances of God, and the means of grace, including the public worship of God (Hebrews 10:25), the ministry of the Word (Acts 2:42), the sacrament of the Lord's Supper (1 Corinthians 11:23-30); searching the Scriptures and meditating thereon (Acts 17:11; 2 Timothy 2:15; 3:14-16); family and private devotions (Deuteronomy 6:6-7; Matthew 6:6).

27.2. SECOND. By avoiding evil of every kind, including:

(1) Taking the name of God in vain (Exodus 20:7; Leviticus 19:12; James 5:12).

(2) Profaning of the Lord's Day by participation in unnecessary secular activities, thereby indulging in practices that deny its sanctity (Exodus 20:8-11; Isaiah 58:13-14; Mark 2:27-28; Acts 20:7; Revelation 1:10).

(3) Sexual immorality, such as premarital or extramarital relations, perversion in any form, or looseness and impropriety of conduct (Exodus 20:14; Matthew 5:27-32; 1 Corinthians 6:9-11; Galatians 5:19; 1 Thessalonians 4:3-7).

(4) Habits or practices known to be destructive of physical and mental well-being. Christians are to regard themselves as temples of the Holy Spirit (Proverbs 20:1; 23:1-3; 1 Corinthians 6:17-20; 2 Corinthians 7:1; Ephesians 5:18).

(5) Quarreling, returning evil for evil, gossiping, slandering, spreading surmises injurious to the good names of others (2 Corinthians 12:20; Galatians 5:15; Ephesians 4:30-32; James 3:5-18; 1 Peter 3:9-10).

(6) Dishonesty, taking advantage in buying and selling, bearing false witness, and like works of darkness (Leviticus 19:10-11; Romans 12:17; 1 Corinthians 6:7-10).

(7) The indulging of pride in dress or behavior. Our people are to dress with the Christian simplicity and modesty that become holiness (Proverbs 29:23; 1 Timothy 2:8-10; James 4:6; 1 Peter 3:3-4; 1 John 2:15-17).

(8) Music, literature, and entertainments that dishonor God (1 Corinthians 10:31; 2 Corinthians 6:14-17; James 4:4).

27.3. THIRD. By abiding in hearty fellowship with the church, not inveighing against but wholly committed to its doctrines and usages and actively involved in its continuing witness and outreach (Ephesians 2:18-22; 4:1-3, 11-16; Philippians 2:1-8; 1 Peter 2:9-10).

NOTES

Chapter 1

1. Sydney E. Ahlstrom, *A Religious History of the American People* (London and New Haven, Conn.: Yale University Press, 1972), 475.

2. Donald F. Durnbaugh, *The Believers' Church: The History and Character of Radical Protestantism* (New York: Macmillan Co., 1968), 32-33.

3. J. B. Chapman, "October Gleanings," *Herald of Holiness*, October 15, 1930, 5; idem, "Dr. Bresee, an Apostolic Leader," *Preacher's Magazine*, December 1938, 2.

4. P. F. Bresee, "Editorial: It Is All Right," *Nazarene Messenger*, January 15, 1902, 6.

5. The analogy is made in Carl Bangs, *Phineas F. Bresee: His Life in Methodism, the Holiness Movement, and the Church of the Nazarene* (Kansas City: Beacon Hill Press of Kansas City, 1995), 282.

Chapter 2

1. *Manual, Church of the Nazarene, 1997—2001* (Kansas City: Nazarene Publishing House, 1997). Paragraphs cited are from this edition.

2. Stan Ingersol, "Christian Baptism and the Early Nazarenes: The Sources That Shaped a Pluralistic Baptismal Tradition," *Wesleyan Theological Journal* 25, No. 2 (fall 1990): 34-35.

3. Maria Harris, *Fashion Me a People* (Louisville, Ky.: John Knox Press, 1989), 77.

4. See the general secretary's report, *Herald of Holiness*, June 1997, special insert, pages not numbered.

5. Clyde E. Fant, *Preaching for Today* (New York: Harper and Row, 1975), 22.

6. Richard Lischer, *A Theology of Preaching* (Nashville: Abingdon Press, 1981), 74.

7. Wesley D. Tracy et al., *The Upward Call: Spiritual Formation and the Holy Life* (Kansas City: Beacon Hill Press of Kansas City, 1994), 133.

8. See the education commissioner's report, *Herald of Holiness*, June 1997, special insert, pages not numbered.

9. Quoted in Donald S. Metz, *MidAmerica Nazarene College: The Pioneer Years, 1966-1991* (Kansas City: Nazarene Publishing House, 1991), 74.

10. Ibid., 46.

11. Charles Wesley, "Help Us to Help Each Other, Lord," in *Wesley Hymns*, comp. Ken Bible (Kansas City: Lillenas Publishing Co., 1982), No. 110.

12. Maxie Dunnam, *Alive in Christ* (Nashville: Abingdon Press, 1982), 113.

13. Ibid., 118. Dunnam is quoting from Malcolm Muggeridge's *Something Beautiful for God*.

14. John Telford, ed., *The Letters of the Rev. John Wesley, A.M.*, 8 vols. (London: Epworth Press, 1960), 1:239.

Chapter 3

1. J. B. Whiteley, *Wesley's England* (London: Epworth Press, 1954), 28.

2. *London Chronicle*, December 17-19, 1772; *Lloyd's Evening Post*, December 21, 1772; *Leeds Mercury*, December 29, 1772.

3. D. D. Thompson, *John Wesley as a Social Reformer* (New York: Eaton and Mains, 1898), 94.

4. *New Castle* (England) *Journal*, March 21, 1767.

5. Thompson, *Wesley a Reformer*, 94.

6. *Leeds Intelligencer*, 1791. Cited in Robert Wearmouth, *Methodism and the Common People of the Eighteenth Century* (London: Epworth Press, 1945), 71-72.

7. *London Chronicle*, September 11, 1762. For more about the social conditions of Wesley's times, see "Economic Policies and Judicial Oppression as Formative Influences on the Theology of John Wesley," by Wesley D. Tracy in *Wesleyan Theological Journal*, spring-fall 1992, 30-56. Also see Wearmouth's book in note 6.

8. *Gentlemen's Magazine*, July 1741.

9. Richard P. Heitzenrater, *Wesley and the People Called Methodist* (Nashville: Abingdon Press, 1995), 80.

10. See Tracy et al., *Upward Call*, 193-200, for more on Wesley's family religion.

11. John Wesley, letter to Frances Godfrey, in Telford, *Letters*, 8:158.

12. John Wesley, letter to William Holland, February 6, 1748, ibid., 2:115.

13. Tracy et al., *Upward Call*, 139. For a fuller treatment of the history and principles of Wesley's Christian Conference, see *Upward Call*, 133-200.

14. Telford, *Letters*, 1:239.

15. *The Works of John Wesley*, 3rd ed., 14 vols. (reprint, Kansas City: Beacon Hill Press of Kansas City, 1978-79), 8:267.

16. Ibid., 7:286-87.

17. *London Chronicle*, January 1761.

18. *Works*, 7:424.

19. Ibid., 8:47.

20. Telford, *Letters*, 5:101-3.

21. Ibid., 4:188.

22. Ibid., 5:215.

23. Henry Bett, *The Spirit of Methodism* (London: Epworth Press, 1937), 123.

24. John Wesley, *Sermons on Several Occasions* (London: Wesleyan Methodist Book Room, n.d.), 4.

25. Ibid., 552.

26. Ibid., 549.

27. Ibid., 556.

28. Albert Outler, *Theology in the Wesleyan Spirit* (Nashville: Tidings, 1975), 45.

29. Durwood Foster, "Wesleyan Theology: Heritage and Task," in *Wesleyan Theology Today*, ed. T. Runyon (Nashville: Kingswood Books, 1985), 31.

30. Bett, *Spirit of Methodism*, 20.

31. John Wesley, *Sermons on Several Occasions*, 297.

32. Outler, *Theology*, 46.

Chapter 4

1. Arthur B. Moss, "Barbara Ruckle Heck," in *The Encyclopedia of World Methodism*, ed. Nolan B. Harmon (Nashville: United Methodist Publishing House, 1974), 1:1103-4.

2. Kenneth B. Bedell, *Yearbook of American and Canadian Churches, 1996* (Nashville: Abingdon, 1996), 250-51.

3. *The Book of Discipline of the United Methodist Church, 1996* (Nashville: The United Methodist Publishing House, 1996), 41-42.

4. Ibid., 43-46.

5. Ibid., 62.

6. Ibid., 71.

7. Ibid., 107-17.

8. A. M. Hills, "The Silver Jubilee Anniversary," *Herald of Holiness*, November 22, 1933, 10.

9. E. F. Walker, "New Denominations," *Nazarene Messenger*, April 1, 1909, 7.

Chapter 5

1. Paul Westphal Thomas and Paul William Thomas, *Days of Our Pilgrimage: History of the Pilgrim Holiness Church* (Marion, Ind.: Wesley Press, 1976), 95; Lee M. Haines and Paul William Thomas, *An Outline History of The Wesleyan Church*, 3rd ed. (Marion, Ind.: Wesley Press, 1985), 126-27.

2. *Yearbook of American and Canadian Churches, 1997*, ed. Kenneth B. Bedell (Nashville: Abingdon Press, 1997), 251, 258; Frank S. Mead and Samuel S. Hill, *Handbook of Denominations in the United States*, 10th ed. (Nashville: Abingdon Press, 1995), 303.

3. Bedell, *Yearbook of Churches, 1997*, 249, 255.

4. Ibid., 250, 257.

5. John W. V. Smith, *The Quest for Holiness and Unity: A Centennial History of the Church of God (Anderson, Ind.)* (Anderson, Ind.: Warner Press, 1980), 37-40, 44-80; *The First Century*,

ed. Barry L. Callen, 2 vols. (Anderson, Ind.: Warner Press, 1979), 1:25-29, 43-54; *An Encyclopedia of Religions in the United States: One Hundred Religious Groups Speak for Themselves,* ed. William B. Williamson (New York: Crossroad, 1992), 80.

6. A. M. Kiergan, *Historical Sketches of the Revival of True Holiness and Local Church Polity from 1865-1916* (Fort Scott, Kans.: Church Advocate and Good Way, n.d.; reprint ca. 1972), 34-42; Clarence Eugene Cowen, *A History of the Church of God (Holiness)* (Overland Park, Kans.: Herald and Banner Press, 1949), 17-32.

7. Charles Edwin Jones, *Black Holiness: A Guide to the Study of Black Participation in Wesleyan Perfectionist and Glossolalic Pentecostal Movements* (Metuchen, N.J.: American Theological Library Association and the Scarecrow Press, 1987), 45-46.

8. Bedell, *Yearbook of Churches, 1997,* 248, 253; D. P. Hollinger, "Christian and Missionary Alliance," in *Dictionary of Christianity in America,* ed. Daniel G. Reid et al. (Downers Grove, Ill.: InterVarsity Press, 1990), 251-52.

Chapter 6

1. Ted A. Campbell, *Christian Confessions* (Louisville, Ky.: Westminster/John Knox Press, 1995), 19.

2. Patrick Henry Reardon, "The Other East," *Books and Culture,* March-April 1996, 7.

3. Letter in G. Williams, *The Orthodox Church of the East in the Eighteenth Century,* 17, quoted in Timothy Kallistos Ware, *The Orthodox Church* (New York: Penguin Books, 1993), 196.

4. Campbell, *Christian Confessions,* 19.

5. Reardon, "The Other East," 6.

6. Ware, *Orthodox Church,* 196.

7. *Manual, Church of the Nazarene, 1997—2001* (Kansas City: Nazarene Publishing House, 1997), 26.

8. Campbell, *Christian Confessions,* 39.

9. *Manual, Church of the Nazarene, 1997—2001,* 26-27, italics added.

10. Ware, *Orthodox Church,* 225.

11. Ibid.

12. Ibid., 229-30.

13. Ibid., 230.

14. Ibid.

15. Ibid., 230-31.

16. *Manual, Church of the Nazarene, 1997—2001,* 27.

17. Ware, *Orthodox Church,* 257.

18. Ibid., 259.

19. Ibid., 219.

20. Campbell, *Christian Confessions,* 48.

21. Ibid.

22. Ware, *Orthodox Church,* 223.

23. Ibid.

24. See Michael J. Christensen, "Theosis and Sanctification: John Wesley's Reformulation of a Patristic Doctrine," *Wesleyan Theological Journal* 31, No. 2 (fall 1996): 72.

25. Ware, *Orthodox Church,* 231.

26. The connection between Wesley's doctrine of perfection and that of the Eastern fathers has been explored by a number of scholars. The following sources are among those recommended for further reading: Paul M. Bassett and William M. Greathouse, *Exploring Christian Holiness,* vol. 2, *The Historical Development* (Kansas City: Beacon Hill Press of Kansas City, 1985); Ted Campbell, *John Wesley and Christian Antiquity* (Nashville: Kingswood Books, 1991); Randy L. Maddox, *Responsible Grace: John Wesley's Practical Theology* (Nashville: Abingdon Press, 1994). Among several useful articles on the subject in the *Wesleyan Theological Journal* are Luke L. Keefer Jr., "John Wesley: Disciple of Early Christianity," vol. 19, No. 1 (spring 1984); John G. Merritt, "Dialogue Within a Tradition: John Wesley and Gregory of Nyssa Discuss Christian Perfection," vol. 22, No. 2 (fall 1987):92-116; and Christensen, see note 24 above.

27. Ware, *Orthodox Church,* 262.

28. Ibid., 278.

29. Ibid., 300.

30. Ibid., 307.

Chapter 7

1. Richard P. McBrien, *Catholicism* (San Francisco: Harper San Francisco, 1989), 3. McBrien cites Ignatius as dying ca. 107. Others date his *Epistle to the Smyrmaeans* at 110 or 120.

2. *Beacon Dictionary of Theology*, ed. Richard S. Taylor (Kansas City: Beacon Hill Press of Kansas City, 1983), 96.

3. Paul L. Williams, *Everything You Always Wanted to Know About the Catholic Church but Were Afraid to Ask for Fear of Excommunication* (New York: Doubleday, 1989), 8.

4. Walter A. Elwell, *Evangelical Dictionary of Theology* (Grand Rapids: Baker Book House, 1984), 1109.

5. Williams, *Everything About the Catholic Church*, 20.

6. Bruce L. Shelley, *Church History in Plain Language* (Waco, Tex.: Word Books, 1982), 296.

7. Elwell, *Evangelical Dictionary of Theology*, 1134.

8. *Fifty Years of Catholic Theology: Conversations with Yves Congar*, ed. Bernard Lauret (London: SCM Press, 1988), 15.

9. Williams, *Everything About the Catholic Church*, 31.

10. Shelley, *Church History in Plain Language*, 479.

11. Williams, *Everything About the Catholic Church*, 67.

12. Oscar Lukefahr, *We Believe . . . A Survey of Catholic Faith* (Liguori, Mo.: Liguori Publications, 1995), 67.

13. Ibid., 68.

14. Ibid., 69.

15. Oscar Lukefahr, *The Privilege of Being Catholic* (Liguori, Mo.: Liguori Publications, 1993), 125.

16. Lukefahr, *We Believe*, 94-95.

17. Ibid., 95.

18. *Manual, Church of the Nazarene, 1997—2001*, par. 800.2, 220.

19. Lukefahr, *We Believe*, 93.

20. Ibid., 97.

21. *The People's Catechism*, ed. Raymond A. Lucker, Patrick J. Brennan, and Michael Leach (New York: Crossroad Publishing Co., 1995), 149.

22. Williams, *Everything About the Catholic Church*, 284, 288.

23. Ibid., 286.

24. Ibid., 117.

25. Ibid.

26. See ibid., 247.

27. Mead and Hill, *Handbook of Denominations*, 270.

Chapter 8

1. Williston Walker, *A History of the Christian Church*, 2nd ed. (New York: Charles Scribner's Sons, 1959), 291-97.

2. Heiko A. Oberman, *Luther: Man Between God and the Devil* (New York: Image Books, 1992), 277-83.

3. Ernest Stoeffler, *The Rise of Evangelical Pietism*, (Leiden: E. J. Brill), 1:965.

4. *Yearbook of American and Canadian Churches, 1996*, ed. Kenneth B. Bedell (Nashville: Abingdon Press, 1996), 2.

5. Martin E. Marty, "Lutheran Churches in America," in Reid et al., *Dictionary of Christianity in America*, 670-74.

6. J. D. Sutherland, "Lutheran World Federation," ibid., 678.

7. See Robert E. Cushman's essay "The Landmarks of the Wesleyan Revival" in his anthology, *Faith Seeking Understanding* (Durham, N.C.: Duke University Press, 1981), 51-52.

Chapter 9

1. A useful survey of Zwingli's career is found in John T. McNeill, *The History and Character of Calvinism* (London: Oxford University Press, 1954), 18-52. The book also contains a minibiography of John Calvin's life and thought.

2. Ulrich Zwingli, *Commentary on True and False Religion* (Durham, N.C.: Labyrinth Press, 1981), 185-97.

3. Ibid., 233-34.

4. McNeill, *History and Character of Calvinism*, 52.

5. Ibid., 208-14.

6. Paul Tillich, *A History of Christian Thought* (New York: Simon and Schuster, 1968), 270.

7. John Calvin, *Institutes of the Christian Religion*, ed. John T. McNeill, trans. Ford Lewis Battle, vol. 2 (Philadelphia: Westminster Press, 1960), 1324-33.

8. McNeill, *History and Character of Calvinism*, 263-66. The definitive biography of Arminius in English is Carl Bangs, *Arminius: A Study in the Dutch Reformation* (Nashville: Abingdon Press, 1971).

9. Bedell, *Yearbook of Churches, 1996*, 94.

10. L. W. Wilshire, "Congregationalism," in Reid et al., *Dictionary of Christianity in America*, 309-11.

11. Bedell, *Yearbook of Churches, 1997*, 257.

12. E. J. Bruins, "Reformed Church in America," in Reid et al., *Dictionary of Christianity in America*, 985-86.

13. A. H. Freundt, "Presbyterian Church in America," ibid., 929-30.

14. "Presbyterian Groups Grow Rapidly in Korea," *Christian Century*, September 25—October 2, 1996, 888.

15. John Wesley, *Works*, 8:284-85.

Chapter 10

1. J. R. H. Moorman, *History of the Church in England*, 3rd ed. (London: Adam and Charles Black, 1976), 355-56.

2. Bedell, *Yearbook of Churches, 1996*, 129, 246, 253.

3. Stephen Neill, *Anglicanism* (London: Penguin Books, 1958), 418.

4. Ibid.

5. Ibid., 424.

6. Ibid., 426.

7. Harmon, *Encyclopedia of World Methodism*, 1:149; *Manual, Pentecostal Church of the Nazarene* (Los Angeles: Nazarene Publishing Co., 1908), 26-27; and *Manual, Church of the Nazarene, 1997—2001*, 27-28.

Chapter 11

1. "The Schleitheim Text," *Gospel Herald*, February 27, 1977, 153-56.

2. Bedell, *Yearbook of Churches, 1997*, 257.

3. Membership statistics for Church of the Brethren and sister churches are from ibid., 253-57.

4. Thomas Hamm, *The Transformation of American Quakerism* (Bloomington, Ind.: Indiana University Press, 1988), 16.

5. Bedell, *Yearbook of Churches, 1997*, 255.

Chapter 12

1. Durnbaugh, *Believers' Church*, 97-99.

2. Ibid., 99.

3. William H. Brackney, "The General Missionary Convention of the Baptist Denomination, 1814-1845: An American Metaphor," *Baptist History*, July 1989, 14.

4. Willis Hubert Porter and Philip E. Jenks, "Baptists," in Williamson, *Encyclopedia of Religions*, 30.

5. M. G. Bell, "Landmark Movement," in Reid et al., *Dictionary of Christianity in America*, 629-30.

6. B. Gray Allison, "Notable Achievements in Missions and Evangelism Since 1845," *Baptist History*, July 1989, 33; Claude L. Howe Jr., "A Portrait of Baptists in America Today," ibid., 50-51; Bedell, *Yearbook of Churches, 1997*, 252.

7. J. Gordon Melton, *Encyclopedia of American Religions*, 2nd ed. (Detroit: Gale Research Co., 1987), 388; Bedell, *Yearbook of Churches, 1997*, 254.

8. Bedell, *Yearbook of Churches, 1997*, 94-95, 256.

9. Melton, *Encyclopedia of American Religions*, 401; Bedell, *Yearbook of Churches, 1997*, 251.

10. Bedell, *Yearbook of Churches, 1997*, 86, 255.

Chapter 13

1. Mark G. Toulouse, *Joined in Discipleship* (St. Louis: Chalice Press, 1992), 27. Quoted without reference.

2. Lester G. McAllister and William E. Tucker, *Journey in Faith: A History of the Christian Church (Disciples of Christ)* (St. Louis: Bethany Press, 1975), 77-79.

3. "The Last Will and Testament of the Springfield Presbytery," in Louis Cochran and Bess White Cochran, *Captives of the Word* (Garden City, N.Y.: Doubleday, 1969), 31.

4. Stephen J. England, *We Disciples* (St. Louis: Christian Board of Publication, 1946), 12.

5. For other summaries of this document, see Cochran and Cochran, *Captives of the Word*, 6-7, and England, *We Disciples*, 14-16.

6. England, *We Disciples*, 18.

7. For a comparative chart of the beliefs and practices of the three churches in this tradition, see Cochran and Cochran, *Captives of the Word*, 254. See Mead and Hill, *Handbook of Denominations*, 94-101, for more statistical and structural detail of the churches in the Restoration Movement.

8. D. Duane Cummins, *A Handbook for Today's Disciples* (St. Louis: Bethany Press, 1981), 23.

9. Ibid., 50-51.

10. Ibid., 51.

11. Ibid., 28.

12. Article XII, *Manual, Church of the Nazarene, 1997—2001*, 32.

13. Article I, ibid., 26.

14. Cummins, *Handbook for Today's Disciples*, 25.

15. Ibid., 46.

16. Ibid.

17. John Wesley, "A Caution Against Bigotry," in *Sermons on Several Occasions*, 547.

Chapter 14

1. An excellent history of the church is Vinson Synan's *Old-Time Power: A History of the Pentecostal Holiness Church* (Franklin Springs, Ga.: Advocate Press, 1973).

2. Bedell, *Yearbook of Churches, 1996*, 254; and International Pentecostal Holiness Church web site, at <http://www.iphc.org/docs/hisherit.html>, March 26, 1997.

3. Bedell, *Yearbook of Churches, 1996*, 251. Also Susie C. Stanley, "Churches of God," in Reid et al., *Dictionary of Christianity in America*, 279. Also the Church of God (Cleveland, Tenn.) web site, at <http://www.mindspring.com/~cog/cog3.htm>, March 31, 1997.

4. William W. Menzies, "The Non-Wesleyan Origins of the Pentecostal Movement," in *Aspects of Pentecostal-Charismatic Origins*, ed. Vinson Synan (Plainfield, N.J.: Logos International, 1975), 90-92.

5. Assemblies of God Pentecostal Fellowship web site, at <http://www.cyberramp.net/~gdm/index.html>, March 27, 1997.

6. International Church of the Foursquare Gospel web site, at <http://www.foursquare.org/detail.html>, March 7, 1997.

7. Les Parrott III and Robin D. Perrin, "The New Denominations," *Christianity Today* (March 11, 1991), 30.

8. Charismatic Episcopal Church web site, at <http://www.iccec.org/info.htm>, March 26, 1997.

9. Ron and Vicki Burks, *Damaged Disciples* (Grand Rapids: Zondervan Publishing House, 1992), 7-8.

10. Robert Digitale, "An Idea Whose Time Has Gone?" *Christianity Today* 34, No. 5 (March 1990): 40.

11. Thomas F. Zimmerman, "Priorities and Beliefs of Pentecostals," *Christianity Today* (September 4, 1981), 36-37.

Chapter 15

1. *Holiness Evangel*, January 1, 1907, 1; and November 15, 1907, 4. Also see the *Pentecostal Advocate*, April 8, 1909, 10.

2. Board of General Superintendents, "The Position of the Church of the Nazarene on Speaking in Tongues," *Herald of Holiness*, October 15, 1976, 5.

3. *Manual, Church of the Nazarene, 1997—2001*, par. 904.10, 350.

4. H. Ray Dunning, *Grace, Faith, and Holiness: A Wesleyan Systematic Theology* (Kansas City: Beacon Hill Press of Kansas City, 1988), 429-77.

5. Ronald M. Enroth, *Churches That Abuse* (Grand Rapids: Zondervan, 1992), 169-72. Enroth refers to Hobart Freeman's Faith Assembly (not associated with the Assemblies of God) in Indiana.

6. Ibid., 26.

7. Ibid., 198.

8. Wesley Tracy, "Abused Believers," *Herald of Holiness*, August 1992, 10.

9. Ibid., 11.

10. Enroth, *Churches That Abuse*, 196. Phil Aguilar is the pastor quoted.

11. See "The Question Box," *Herald of Holiness*, October 1997, 34.

12. "The Position . . . ," *Herald of Holiness*, October 15, 1976, 5.